FAMILY KNITS

100 IDEES
BALLANTINE BOOKS · NEW YORK

Conceived, designed and produced by
Conran Octopus Limited
37 Shelton Street
London WC2 9HN

Editor: Diana Mansour
Contributing Editor: Philippa Wolledge
Art Editor: Caroline Murray
Designer: Paul Cooper
Illustrators: Prue Brucknall, Alison Leggate
and Colin Woodman
Production: Louise Barratt

The editors would like to thank Marilyn Wilson and Penny Hill for their assistance.

Library of Congress Catalog Card Number 87-91501

ISBN: 0-345-34719-6

Manufactured in Hong Kong

* First American Edition: February 1988

10 9 8 7 6 5 4 3 2 1

CONTENTS

INTRODUCTION

Most knitters have faced this problem at one time or another – you have seen an attractive pattern and knitted it for one member of the family, only to find that everyone else is feeling left out and is clamoring for you to make another and another. Often the pattern is only available in a limited size range, causing great disappointment to the excluded ones. If, on the other hand, it can be adjusted, do you then start on a production line of identical garments, or cry off, making excuses about lack of time? Here is a book which will solve all your problems and delight your family.

Many of the designs featured are really families of patterns, subtly or boldly varied to give interest to the knitter and individuality to the wearer. In some cases, such as the lovely summery cotton sweaters on page 12, it is only the colors which change, but in others, such as the Scandinavian style group of patterns shown on page 52, there is a complete range of patterns. They have totally different motifs but all are carefully coordinated in color and design to make a clear statement of family style.

The cold-weather knits on page 14 include several styles, ranging from a parka with a drawstring waist to a jacket with a roll collar, both for an adult or teenager, and a child's jacket in a two-tone pattern. The underlying unity comes from the fact that they are all composed of two reversible layers of cozy mohair, knitted in contrasting colors for added interest and detailing.

Men enjoy identifying with their children just as much as women, and there are several delightful patterns designed to be worn by father and child (though many could also be worn by mother and child), such as the negative/positive sweaters on page 24, or the lightning flash design on page 42.

The patterns vary considerably in complexity: some of them, such as the Paisley pattern sweaters on page 60, are for rather more experienced knitters, while others, such as the delightful set of animal hoods and sweaters on page 28, are comparatively quick and simple to make. The set of gym/ballet accessories on page 36 are so easy that they could probably be knitted by the young wearer herself.

All the designs have this in common: they combine a sense of family fun with a very French feeling for style. These are patterns which will make knitting enjoyable and rewarding – for you and your family.

BASIC ESSENTIALS

It is assumed that people using this book will have mastered the basic skills of knitting, but some of the designs may include techniques with which you are unfamiliar, in which case the following instructions show how they should be tackled. The ages quoted for the children's knits are only a general guide, since children of a given age can vary so much in size, so check the measurement diagram before embarking on a pattern, bearing in mind that the garment should be between 2 and 4in (5 and 10cm) wider than the chest measurement of the person, for ease of movement.

YARNS
Some of the French yarns originally used for these patterns are not readily available outside France, or must be obtained by mail order or from specialist shops. Where this is the case, suppliers or substitute yarns which are more easily available are listed on pages 78-80.

ABBREVIATIONS
The standard abbreviations used in this book are listed below. Any other abbreviations, used for a particular design, are given with the instructions.
k = knit
p = purl
st(s) = stitch(es)
st st = stockinette stitch
rev st st = reverse stockinette stitch (using p side as right side)
g st = garter stitch
rep = repeat
beg = beginning
patt = pattern
yfd = yarn forward
yrn = yarn round needle
tog = together
SKPO = slip 1, k 1, pass slipped st over
SKTPO = slip 1, k 2 tog, pass slipped st over
tbl = through back of loop (or loops)
kw = knitwise
pw = purlwise
cont = continue
rem = remaining
alt = alternate
foll = follow(s)(ing)
kfb (or pfb) = k (or p) into front and back of next st

inc = increase
dec = decrease
cm = centimetres
in = inches
s c = single crochet

GAUGE
This is the most important part of any garment, yet it is the aspect which most knitters ignore. The designer has worked out the instructions on the basis of a particular gauge and unless yours is exactly the same the finished garment will not be the correct size or shape, neither will the parts fit correctly together. The correct gauge is given with each design and also the number of stitches which you should cast on to work a sample; by doing this you will be able to check that your gauge is correct before starting the work and this will avoid disappointment later. Knit the sample in the pattern given, or in stockinette stitch if this is the basic pattern used; continue until the sample measures 5in (12cm) then bind off and measure the gauge.

If your gauge is not exactly right, try again using larger or smaller needles as necessary in order to obtain the correct gauge.

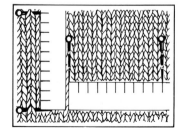

If you have more stitches to 4in (10cm) than stated you are working too tightly and you should try larger needles; if you have fewer stitches you are working too loosely and you should try smaller needles. Use needles which produce the correct gauge for the main parts of the garment, making corresponding alterations in the needle size(s) given for other parts such as ribbed borders or cuffs.

SIDES OF WORK
The first row worked after casting-on is always the right side unless otherwise stated. The expression 'front of work' refers to the side on which you are actually knitting and 'back' to the side away from you; these should not be confused with the terms 'right side' and 'wrong side' of work.

INCREASES AND DECREASES
To increase at the beginning of a row, either cast on a stitch or work into the front and back of the first stitch. To increase at the end of a row, work into the front and back of the last stitch. In this way it is easier to match the increases at the sides and thus make a neater seam. To decrease at the beginning of a row, either bind off a stitch or work SKPO. At the end of a row, knit the last two stitches together.

DOUBLE YARN
For some designs yarn has to be used double. Using the two balls separately can result in an uneven appearance and it is easy to miss one of the strands. To avoid these difficulties, take a ball of the yarn and wind it into two balls of the same size, then rewind them together to form a double thickness ball.

SWISS DARNING
This is a popular and simple way of decorating garments by covering the stockinette stitch, one stitch at a time, with a different color or colors. The effect is the same as if the colors had been knitted in but it is much

easier to work. The method is used for embroidering the lightning flash design of the father's and child's sweaters which are feature on pages 42-5. It is also used for the small diamonds seen on the child's jacket in Snow Set on page 14. In both these cases, the background patterning must first be knitted and cannot be embroidered in Swiss darning. This also applies to the designs shown on the sweaters for Tweedy Family, page 70, and Negative/Positive, page 24, since Fair Isle has a different gauge.

Swiss darning can be worked either horizontally or vertically, whichever fits in most easily with the motif or pattern. If you are working isolated dots, simply carry the yarn across the back of the work as you would if knitting a Fair Isle pattern. Use a blunt-ended wool needle and, if you are using scrap-bag yarns, make sure that they are thick enough to cover the knitted stitches.

HORIZONTAL TECHNIQUE
Thread your needle and bring it out at the bottom right-hand corner of the motif, at the base of the first knitted stitch to be covered. Working from right to left, insert the needle behind the stitch immediately above.

Pull the yarn through, then insert the needle back through the base of the first stitch and bring it out at the base of the stitch immediately to the left.

Pull the yarn through, covering the first stitch, then work from left to right along the row.

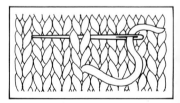

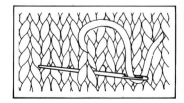

VERTICAL TECHNIQUE

This is worked more like chain-stitch embroidery, which Swiss darning closely resembles. Begin at the bottom, as for the horizontal technique, bringing the yarn through at the base of the first stitch and taking the needle from right to left behind the stitch above. Pull the yarn through and then insert the needle vertically behind the first stitch, as shown. Pull the yarn through to cover the first stitch and continue upwards.

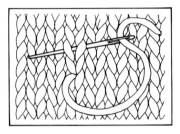

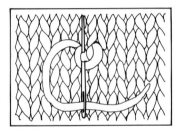

JACQUARD KNITTING

A few of the designs in this book are examples of the technique known as jacquard. The method of working is quite different from traditional Fair Isle in which two or more colors are carried across the row and used when needed. Jacquard designs either have motifs which may be small or large and are isolated against a background color or else they have large panels or geometric shapes worked in various colors. In all these cases it is necessary to use separate balls of color for each of the different motifs and, if these are large, a separate ball of the background color is also needed for the stitches on each side. Join on the balls where necessary by making a single knot into the previous stitch; afterwards these knots can be unpicked and the ends darned in securely.

To avoid using whole balls of yarn wind off a small ball for each section; it is more convenient to wind them onto strips of cardboard. Cut a slit in the card so that the yarn can be passed through the slit when it is not being used. It will then hang without becoming entangled. All the spare colors are kept on the wrong side of the work and it is essential each time you begin with a new color to pick it up from underneath the color previously used so that it passes right around the previous color. This will avoid holes forming in the work.

The technique requires practice to avoid the edges of the various sections becoming too loose.

FINISHING

Before sewing the garment together you may need to press the work, but check by consulting the ball-band. This will show by use of the conventional signs whether the yarn is one which can be pressed or not. Yarns that are composed of 100 per cent wool or 100 per cent cotton may be pressed by the method explained below but *do not* press garments knitted in garter stitch or in any pattern such as cable or those with a raised texture, or in any type of rib, as pressing would spoil the appearance. In these cases (also in the case of yarns where the actual knitting cannot be pressed) it is advisable to press the seams; again with reference to the ball-band, use either a warm iron and damp cloth or a cool iron and dry cloth and press very lightly using only the point of the iron.

If the yarn and the pattern permits whole sections to be pressed, blocking is a simple way of putting the pieces under a very slight tension during pressing. Fold a large towel or blanket to make a thick ironing pad, then lay the piece of knitting right side down on the pad. If there is a measurement diagram, check this as you pin the piece out, pulling it back into shape if it has become distorted. For a back or front, start by pinning at the widest point, which is generally the chest measurement. Push the pins in right up to the head and position them about ½in (1cm) apart all the way around the garment except at ribbed cuffs and hems, which are never pressed.

When the piece is pinned out, cover it with a clean cloth (damp or dry according to the instructions on the ball band): never put the iron directly on the knitting. Press very lightly, lifting the iron up and putting it down on new sections.

SEAMING

There are several methods of seaming and some are explained below. For most of the garments in this book the backstitch method is preferable, and it has the decided advantage of disguising any uneven edges and hiding the shapings such as shoulder binding off. Where a garment is made in garter stitch the flat seam method may be used instead; the various panels of the child's sweater shown on page 64 are also joined with a flat seam, these seams being afterwards covered by lines of embroidery. Hems and facings should be slip-stitched in place as shown below. For all seams use a blunt-ended wool needle or tapestry needle; this will avoid splitting the yarn – and your fingers!

METHOD 1 BACK-STITCH SEAM

Place the two pieces to be joined with right sides together and begin sewing at the right-hand end of the seam, securing the end of the yarn with two stitches, one on top of the other. Push the needle through both layers and bring it up to the top again. Push the needle in again at the starting

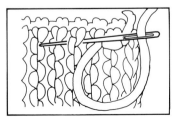

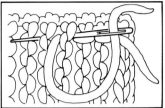

point and bring it out a little further from the point where you last brought it out to make one back-stitch. Continue backstitching to the end of the seam.

METHOD 2 FLAT SEAM

Start with right sides together and two stitches, as for the back-stitch seam. Carefully matching rows or stitches, and pushing the needle through vertically for greater accuracy, join the seam with a running stitch effect.

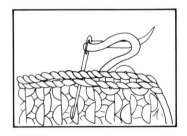

METHOD 3 INVISIBLE SEAMING

Place the two pieces right side up and side by side, matching the rows and edge stitches. Secure the end of the yarn at the bottom right-hand edge and pick up the matching stitch on the left-hand edge. Pull the yarn through tightly, then return to the right-hand edge and pick up the stitch on the next row up.

HEADS IN THE CLOUDS

On course for the moon, this father and son (or it could equally well be mother and daughter) wear easy-to-knit sweaters featuring a subtle design showing the moon shrouded in clouds. The sweater has a straight, loose shape, with hems instead of the more usual bands of ribbing at the cuffs and lower edge, and with a slash neck. The back and sleeves are worked in varying shades of gray lightened with ecru. If gray skies don't appeal to you, you could use the same motif but switch to a mixture of reds and wines, or alternatively rose pinks, dusty blues and pale yellows, transforming the moonlit scene to a stormy sunset or a gentle sunrise.

CHECKLIST

Materials
Georges Picaud Shetland: 1 (2) balls of No 62, dark gray; 2 (3) balls of No 10, light gray; 2 (4) balls of No 8, medium gray, and 1 (4) balls of No 39, ecru. Orient Express: 1 (1) ball in No 4, gold. Pair of double-pointed needles size 7; circular needle size 7; medium-size crochet hook (child's version only).

Sizes
Two sizes, one adult's and one child's, to fit a child aged 4 years, or an adult size 38/40in (97/102cm) chest.

Stitches used
St st, patt, worked from charts.
Use separate balls or short lengths of yarn for each of the sections shown on chart, taking care to wind yarns round each other when changing color. The back is worked in stripes to match those on the front. The stripes are made by alternating 1 row in each color. Use the double-pointed needles or the circular needle to avoid cutting the yarn, then always work from the side where you find the color you need. The yarn is used double throughout.

Gauge
Over st st with yarn used double, 18 sts and 27 rows to 4in (10cm).

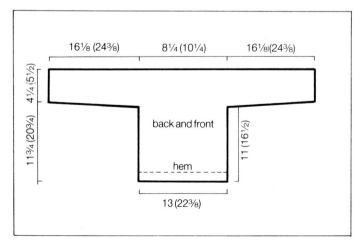

CHILD'S SWEATER — front

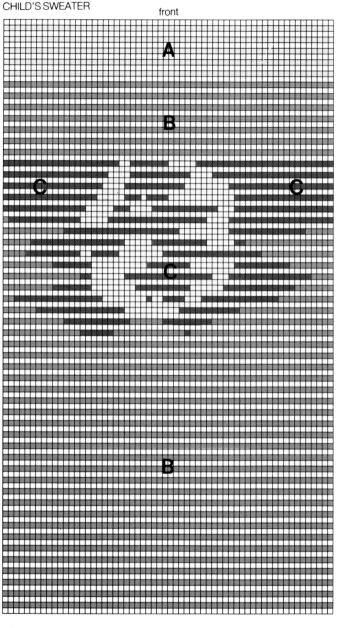

KEY
A = 1 row light gray, 1 row ecru
B = 1 row medium gray, 1 row ecru
C = 1 row dark gray, 1 row ecru
⊡ = gold

ADULT'S SWEATER   front

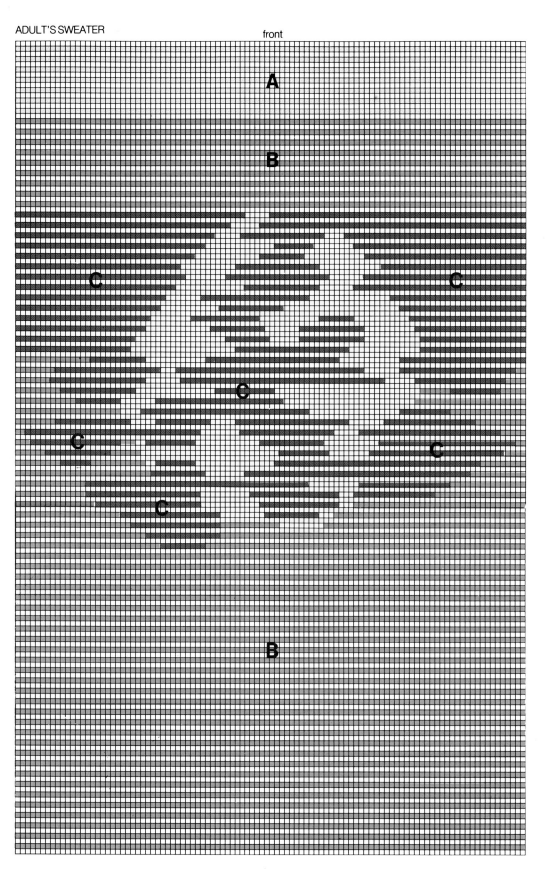

INSTRUCTIONS

▦ **Back** Use the yarn double. With double-pointed needles and medium gray, cast on 60 (102) sts for lower edge and work 2 rows st st for hem.

▦ Cont in st st, alternating 1 row medium gray and 1 row ecru until work measures 11(16½)in/(28,42cm).

▦ Alternating 1 row ecru and 1 row dark gray, work 12 (32) rows and *at the same time* at the 1st (11th) row cast on extra sts for sleeves, as foll, changing to circular needle for the extra sts: *for child's sweater* cast on 21 sts at beg of next 6 rows; *for adult's sweater* cast on 4 sts at beg of next 12 rows and 12 sts at beg of foll 10 rows, 186 (270) sts.

▦ Work 13 (18) rows, alternating 1 row ecru and 1 row medium gray, then cont with ecru and light gray until work measures 16⅛(26⅜)in/(41,67cm) from beg Bind off the 186 (270) sts.

▦ **Front** Foll the instructions for the back until work measures 7⅞(11½)in/(20,29.5cm).

▦ Foll chart, commence moon motif as foll:

▦ *1st row* K 41 (65) **B**, 2 (7) **C**, 17 (30) **B**.

▦ Cont in patt as now set to end of motif, then finish with stripes to match the back.

▦ **Finishing** Join shoulder and upper sleeve seams of back and front for 16⅛(24⅜)in/(41,62cm), leaving 8¼(10¼)in/(21,26cm) free at the center for neck.

▦ Join side and sleeve seams. Turn up the hem at base of back and front.

▦ Make a ¾in (2cm) hem on sleeves. Make a narrow hem round neck edge of adult's sweater. For the child's sweater, work a row of s c round the neck edge with ecru.

YOUNG SHRIMPERS

This lovely set of holiday sweaters is knitted in a soft cotton – ideal for those overcast days that are perfect for shrimping, and just right for evening wear in warmer climates. Back, front and sleeves are all divided in half at the start of the raglan armholes and are completed separately, which makes the color changes much simpler and gives a well-shaped yoke. In an easy-to-knit mixture of rib and stockinette stitch, the basic sweater covers an age range from three to fifteen (check the schema for actual sizes).

CHECKLIST

Materials
Coton Sophie Desroches: 5 (6-7-8) balls in either blue, mustard, pale gray or beige = A, and 1 ball in each of four other colors. Using the picture as a guide, choose your own arrangement of colors and mark them as folls: B is used for the stripe on the right front yoke and for front of left sleeve; C is used for top of right front yoke and a stripe on each sleeve; D is used for stripe on left front yoke and for front half of right sleeve, and E is used for top of left front yoke and a stripe on each sleeve. Colors used for the original sweaters were: No 3214, sky blue; No 3070, mustard; No 3354, gray; No 3001, straw yellow; No 3212, clear blue; No 3020, salmon; No 3380, turquoise; No 3034, gray brown; No 3011, khaki; No 3242, dark green; No 3024, rust, and No 3341, mid green. Pair each of needles size 1 and 2.

Sizes
Four sizes, to fit ages 3 to 4 (6 to 7 – 9 to 11 – 13 to 15) years. Actual measurements shown on diagram.

Stitches used
Single rib; st st.

Gauge
Over st st using larger needles, 29 sts and 40 rows to 4in (10cm). Work a sample on 35 sts.

INSTRUCTIONS

▦ **Front** With smaller needles and **A** cast on 91 (101-113-123) sts and work in k 1, p 1 rib.

▦ ** *1st row* (right side) P 1, * *k 1, p 1; rep from* * to end.

▦ *2nd row* K 1, * p 1, k 1; rep from * to end. Rep these 2 rows until work measures 2(2⅜-2⅜-2¾)in/ (5, 6, 6, 7cm) from beg, ending with 1st rib row. **

▦ *Inc row* Rib 9 (6-2-5), [inc in next st, rib 17 (10-8-6)] 4 (8-12-16) times, inc in next st, rib 9 (6-2-5). 96 (110-126-140) sts. Change to larger needles and work in st st; cont without shaping until work measures 8⅝(10⅝-12¼-13¾)in/(22,27,31,35cm) from beg, ending with a p row.

▦ **Raglan Shaping** *1st row* Bind off 2 (3-5-6), k until there are 46 (52-58-64)sts on right needle, leave these on a holder, k rem 48 (55-63-70) sts. Cont on this group of sts and bind off 2 (3-5-6) sts at beg of foll row. Change to **B**.

▦ *3rd row* K without shaping.

▦ *4th row* K 1, p 2 tog, p to last 3 sts, p 2 tog tbl, k 1.

▦ *5th row* K without shaping.

▦ *6th row* K 1, p to last st k 1. Rep last 4 rows twice more. Change to **C**. Rep from 3rd to 6th rows inclusive 11 (13-15-17) times more. K 1 row then on foll row work dec at raglan edge only. 17 (19-21-23) sts. Change to smaller needles and work 6 (8-8-10) rows in k 1, p 1 rib..

▦ Bind off loosely in rib. With wrong side facing rejoin **A** to other group of 46 (52-58-64) sts, p to end. Change to **D** and cont as on first half of front for next 12 rows then change to **E** and complete as on first half.

▦ **Back** Work exactly as given for front; colors used for right front will thus be used on left back and vice versa.

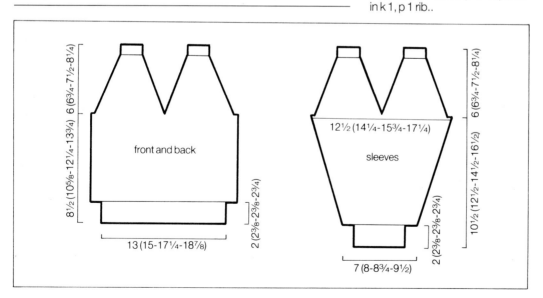

8½ (10⅝-12¼-13¾) | 6 (6¾-7½-8¼)

front and back

13 (15-17¼-18⅞)

2 (2⅜-2⅜-2¾)

12½ (14¼-15¾-17¼)

sleeves

10½ (12½-14½-16½) | 6 (6¾-7½-8¼)

2 (2⅜-2⅜-2¾)

7 (8-8¾-9½)

▦ **Sleeves** With smaller needles and **A** cast on 47 (51-53-57) sts and work as for back ribbing from ** to **.

▦ *Inc row* Rib 5 (4-1-4), [inc in next st, rib 8 (6-4-3)] 4 (6-10-12) times, inc in next st, rib 5 (4-1-4). 52 (58-64-70) sts.

▦ Change to larger needles and work in st st but inc 1 st at both ends of every foll 6th row 1 (3-7-9) times then every foll 4th row 19 (20-19-20) times. Cont on 92 (104-116-128) sts until work measures 10⅝(12⅝-14½-16½)in/(22,32,37,42cm) from beg, ending with a p row.

▦ **Raglan Shaping** *1st row* Bind off 2 (3-5-6), k until there are 44 (49-53-58) sts on right needle, leave these on a holder, k rem 46 (52-58-64) sts. Cont on this group of sts and bind off 2 (3-5-6) sts at beg of foll row. Change to **C**. Rep from 3rd to 6th rows of raglan shaping on front 3 times. Change

to **B** and cont as folls: Rep from 3rd to 6th rows 11 (12-11-13) times more. 16 (19-25-26) sts.

▦ *For 1st size* work 1 row then on foll row dec at raglan edge only; *for 2nd size* work 5 rows straight then rep 4th row; *for 3rd size* work the decs at each end of every foll 6th row 3 times; *for 4th size* work the decs at each end of every foll 6th row twice, work 5 rows then dec at raglan edge only on foll row.

▦ *For all sizes* change to smaller

needles and cont on rem 15 (17-19-21) sts working in rib for 6 (8-8-10) rows then bind off loosely in rib.

▦ With wrong side facing rejoin **A** to other group of 44 (49-53-58) sts, p to end. Complete as for first half of sleeve using **E** for next 12 rows and **D** for remainder.

▦ **Finishing** Join seams along center front and back and center of each sleeve. Join raglan seams. Join side and sleeve seams.

SNOW SET

Marvelous mohair is ideal for the snow – so light, yet so beautifully warm. To emphasize its wonderful cold-beating qualities, each item of this outdoor set is made in two thicknesses, using contrasting colors. After it is made up, each jacket is thus completely reversible, with cuffs turned back to show the contrast. Photographed on the ski slopes of Couchevel in the French alps, these colorful clothes are all easy to make.

JACKET WITH ROLL COLLAR

CHECKLIST

Materials
*Anny Blatt Soft' Anny, Kid Mohair: 17 balls of No 1602, mulberry (**A**), and 17 balls of No 1382, olive (**B**). Pair of needles size 8; large size crochet hook for making up.*

Size
One size only, to fit 32/38in (82/97cm) bust. Actual measurements shown on diagram.

Stitches used
St st; double rib; slip st (in crochet).

Gauge
Over st st using needles given, 15 sts and 24 rows to 4in (10cm). Work a sample on 20 sts.

INSTRUCTIONS

FIRST SECTION

▦ **Back** Using **A**, cast on 94 sts and work in st st. Cont until work measures 22¾in (58cm) from beg, ending with a p row.

▦ **Armhole Shaping** Bind off 3 sts at beg of next 2 rows and 1 st at beg of next 4 rows. Cont on rem 84 sts until work measures 33⅞in (86cm) from beg, ending with a p row.

▦ **Shoulder Shaping** Bind off 7 sts at beg of next 6 rows and 9 sts at beg of next 2 rows. Bind off rem 24 sts for back neck.

▦ **Right Front** Using **A** cast on 60 sts and work in st st. Cont until work measures 12⅝in (32cm) from beg, ending with a p row.

▦ **Pocket Opening** *1st row* K 30, turn and cont on these sts for front section leaving rem 30 sts of side section on a spare needle. Work a further 7½in (19cm)

ending with a k row. Cut yarn and rejoin to 30 sts of side section, k to end. Work 7½in (19cm) on these sts ending with a k row.

▦ *Next row* P 30 sts of side section then p 30 sts of front section. Cont on 60 sts until work matches back to armhole, ending with a k row.

▦ **Armhole Shaping** Bind off 3 sts at beg of next row and dec 1 st at same edge every other row, twice. Cont on rem 55 sts until work matches back to shoulder, ending at side edge.

▦ **Shoulder Shaping** Bind off 7 sts at beg of next row and next 2 alt rows and 9 sts at same edge on next alt row.

▦ Cont on rem 25 sts for collar. Inc 1 st at shaped edge on every foll 4th row 4 times then cont on 29 sts until work measures 3½in (9cm) from beg of collar ending at shaped edge. Bind off 6 sts at beg of next row and then every other row 3 times. Work 1 row and then bind off rem 5 sts.

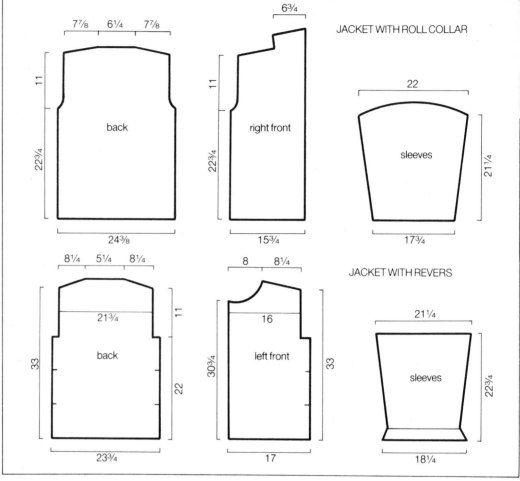

JACKET WITH ROLL COLLAR

JACKET WITH REVERS

Left Front Work as for right front reversing all shapings.

Sleeves Using **A** cast on 68 sts and work in st st. Cont until piece measures 4in (10cm) from beg then inc 1 st at both ends of next row then every foll 14th row 7 times more. Cont on 84 sts until work measures 21¼in (54cm) from beg.

Top Shaping Bind off 3 sts at beg of next 2 rows, 4 sts at beg of next 4 rows and 6 sts at beg of next 2 rows. Bind off rem 50 sts.

Pocket Borders With right side of work facing and using **A**, pick up and k 38 sts along front edge of pocket opening on right front.

1st row (wrong side) P 2, * k 2, p 2; rep from * to end.

2nd row K 2, * p 2, k 2; rep from * to end. Rep these 2 rows until border measures 1in (2.5cm) then bind off in rib. Work similar border on left front pocket opening.

SECOND SECTION

Work all parts as for first section but using **B**.

Finishing For each section join shoulder seams, sew in sleeves then join side and sleeve seams. Join bound-off edges of collar and sew inner edge along back neck easing it to fit. Neatly sew ends of pocket border in place. Slip one section inside the other, having both wrong sides tog. Working on

wrong side and using the crochet hook, slip-st the sections tog at top and bottom of opening. Working on right side join the sections on all outer edges with a

row of slip sts, using the crochet hook. Hold the 2 thicknesses tog by sewing along both shoulder seams.

JACKET WITH REVERS

CHECKLIST

Materials
Bouton d'Or 100 per cent Mohair Gratté: *700g of mustard* (**A**), *and 700g of mint* (**B**). *Pair of needles size 10½.*

Size
One size only, to fit 32/38in (82/97cm) bust. Actual measurements shown on diagram.

Stitch used
St st.

Gauge
Over st st using needles given, 12 sts and 16 rows to 4in (10cm). Work a sample on 16 sts.

INSTRUCTIONS

FIRST SECTION

Back Using **A**, cast on 72 sts and work in st st. Cont until work measures 22in (56cm) from beg, ending with a p row.

Armhole Shaping Bind off 3 sts at beg of next 2 rows then cont on rem 66 sts until work measures 33in (84cm) from beg, ending with a p row.

Shoulder and Neck Shaping Bind off 8 sts at beg of next 2 rows.

3rd row Bind off 8, k until there are 11 sts on right needle, leave these for right back, bind off next 12 sts, k to end. Cont on 19 sts now rem at end of needle for left back. Bind off 8 sts at beg of next row and 2 sts at neck edge on foll row. Bind off rem 9 sts to complete shoulder slope. Rejoin yarn to neck edge of right back sts, bind off 2, p to end. Bind off rem 9 sts.

Left Front Using **A** cast on 52 sts and work in st st. Cont until work measures 22in (56cm) from beg, ending with a p row.

Armhole Shaping Bind off 3 sts at beg of next row then cont on rem 49 sts until work measures 30¾in (78cm) from beg, ending at front edge after a k row.

Neck and Shoulder Shaping Bind off 15 sts at beg of next row, then 5 sts every other row, once; and 2 sts every other row, once; then 1 st every other row, twice. Now keeping neck edge straight bind off for shoulder 8 sts at beg of next row and next alt row, work 1 row then bind off rem 9 sts.

Right Front Work as for left front reversing all shapings.

Sleeves Using **A** cast on 55 sts and work in st st but dec 1 st at both ends of every foll 4th row twice. Cont on 51 sts until work measures 4¾in (12cm) from beg; inc 1 st at both ends of next row then every foll 10th row 3 times, then every foll 8th row 3 times more. Cont on 65 sts until work measures 22¾in (58cm) from beg. Bind off all sts.

SECOND SECTION

Work all parts as for first section but using **B**.

Finishing For each section join shoulder seams; sew bound-off sleeve edges to armhole sides and armhole bind-off to last 4 rows of sleeves. Join sleeve seams. On each side edge put markers 7⅞in (20cm) from lower edge and 7⅛in (18cm) higher, to mark pocket openings. Join side seams above and below openings. Place one jacket inside the other having both right sides tog. Join along front and neck edges and along edges of pocket openings. Turn right sides out. Working from inside and using the crochet hook, slip-st sections tog at upper and lower levels of pocket openings for 7⅞in (20cm) from sides and slip-st vertically to form pockets. On outside neatly sew the sections tog along lower edges and edges of sleeves. Hold thicknesses tog by sewing along shoulder seams.

PARKA

CHECKLIST

Materials

Laine Plassard Florès: *14 balls of No 7, rust* (**A**), *and 14 balls of No 21, pink* (**B**). *Pair of needles size 8; large size crochet hook for making up. An open-ended 21in (70cm) zipper for front opening and 2 ordinary 5in (13cm) zipper for pockets.*

Size

One size only, to fit 32/38in (82/97cm) bust. Actual measurements shown on diagram.

Stitches used

St st; slip-st *(in crochet).*

Gauge

Over st st, using needles given, 16 sts and 24 rows to 4in (10cm). Work a sample on 20 sts.

INSTRUCTIONS

FIRST SECTION

▦ **Back** Using **A** cast on 100 sts and work in st st. Cont until work measures 19¾in (50cm) from beg, ending with a p row.

▦ **Armhole Shaping** Bind off 3 sts at beg of next 2 rows and 2 sts at beg of next 2 rows. Cont on rem 90 sts until work measures 30¾in (78cm) from beg, ending with a p row.

▦ **Shoulder Shaping** Bind off 8 sts at beg of next 8 rows. Bind off rem 26 sts for back neck.

▦ **Right Front** Using **A** cast on 52 sts and work in st st; cont until work measures 6¼in (16cm) from beg, ending with a p row.

▦ **Pocket Opening** *1st row* K 32, turn and cont on these sts for front section leaving rem 20 sts of side section on a spare needle. Dec 1 st at beg of next row and at same edge on next 17 rows; you have ended at the opening after a k row.

▦ Cut yarn and leave rem 14 sts on a spare needle. With right side facing rejoin yarn to 20 sts of side section, k to end. Inc 1 st at end of next row and at same edge on next 17 rows; you have ended at side edge after a k row and there are 38 sts on needle.

▦ *20th row* P 38 then p 14 sts of front section. Cont on 52 sts until work measures 19¾in (50cm) from beg, ending with a k row.

▦ **Armhole Shaping** Bind off 3 sts at beg of next row and 2 sts at same edge every other row once. Cont on rem 47 sts until work measures 28¼in (72cm) from beg, end at front edge.

▦ **Neck and Shoulder Shaping** Bind off 3 sts at beg of next row, 2 sts at same edge on next 5 alt rows and 1 st on next 2 alt rows. Now keeping neck edge straight bind off for shoulder 8 sts at beg of next row and next 2 alt rows, work 1 row then bind off rem 8 sts.

▦ **Left Front** Work as for right front reversing pocket opening and all shapings.

▦ **Sleeves** Using **A** cast on 72 sts and work in st st; inc 1 st at both ends of every foll 12th row 9 times then cont on 90 sts until work measures 21¼in (54cm) from beg.

▦ **Top Shaping** Bind off 3 sts at beg of next 2 rows, 5 sts at beg of next 4 rows and 6 sts at beg of next 2 rows. Bind off rem 52 sts.

▦ **Hood** Using **A** cast on 60 sts and work in st st for 19¾in

(50cm). Bind off.

SECOND SECTION

▦ Work all parts as for first section but using **B**.

▦ **Finishing** For each section join shoulder seams, sew in sleeves then join side and sleeve seams. Fold hood in half and join one side of row ends forming upper seam. Sew hood to neck edges. Place one section inside the other having the p sides tog. Join sections around lower edges of main part and sleeves with a row of slip st, using crochet hook. Join front edges of hood in same way. Sew open-ended zipper between the 2 thicknesses along front edges leaving last ¾in (2cm) open at neck edge and at waistline. Leave an opening for the depth of 4 rows to allow cord to be passed through. Slip-st front edges above top of zipper.

▦ Sew short zippers to pocket openings between the 2 sections. Slip-st the sections tog on inside of openings to form pockets. To make cord work a length of crochet chain 35½in (90cm) long, using **A**, then cont for same length in **B**; work back along the chain in slip st, matching colors.

▦ At waistline backstitch through both thicknesses 4 rows apart for casing and thread cord through.

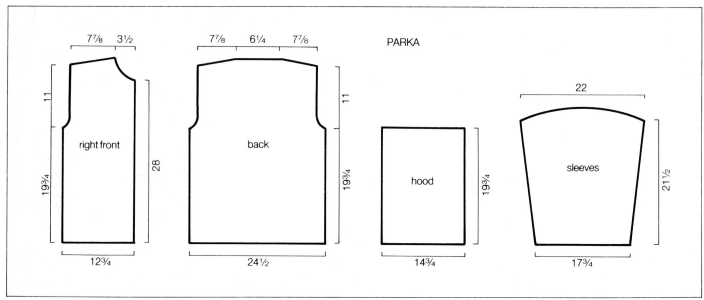

PARKA

right front — 7⅞ · 3½ · 11 · 19¾ · 28 · 12¾

back — 7⅞ · 6¼ · 7⅞ · 11 · 19¾ · 24½

hood — 19¾ · 14¾

sleeves — 22 · 21½ · 17¾

CHILD'S JACKET

CHECKLIST

Materials
Berger du Nord Kid Mohair: 8 (8-9) balls of No 7991, bright blue (A); 6 (6-7) balls of No 8245, dark green (B), and 2 (2-3) balls of No 8250, green (C). Pair of size 5 needles; 8 buttons.

Sizes
Three sizes, to fit ages 6 (8-10) years. Actual measurements shown on diagram.

Stitches used
Single rib; st st.

Gauge
Over st st and using needles given, 16 sts and 23 rows to 4in (10cm). Work a sample on 24 sts.

Note *Section 1 is worked entirely in A and has patch pockets. Section 2 is worked in B with zigzag panels worked in C from chart; the small diamonds in A and C are embroidered afterwards by the Swiss darning method described on page 6.*

See instructions for arrangement of patt on each section. Arrow shows center st for back sleeves and hood.

INSTRUCTIONS

FIRST SECTION

▦ **Back** Using **A** cast on 67 (73-79) sts and work in st st. Cont until work measures 21¼(22¾, 24½)in/(54,58,62cm) from beg.
▦ **Shoulder Shaping** Bind off 7 (8-9) sts at beg of next 4 rows and 8 sts at beg of next 2 rows. Bind off rem 23 (25-27) sts for back neck.

▦ **Left Front** Using **A** cast on 35 (38-41) sts and work in st st. Cont until work measures 19¾(20¾,22⅜)in/(50,53,57cm) from beg ending with a k row.
▦ **Neck and Shoulder Shaping** Bind off 5 (6-7) sts at beg of next

| centre stitch
Work the zigzag patt during the course of the work and emboider the diamonds afterwards in Swiss darning.

row, 2 sts at same edge every other row, twice; and 1 st every other row 4 times. Now bind off for shoulder 7 (8-9) sts at beg of next row and next alt row, work 1 row then bind off rem 8 sts.

▦ **Right Front** Work as for left front reversing all shapings.

▦ **Sleeves** Using **A** cast on 45 (49-53) sts and work in st st but inc 1 st at both ends of every foll 10th row 2 (5-8) times then every foll 8th row 6 (3-0) times. Cont on 61 (65-69) sts until work measures 13⅜(14½,15¾)in/(34,37,40cm) from beg. Bind off all sts.

▦ **Hood** Beg at top edge cast on

61 (65-69) sts and work in st st; cont until work measures 9(9½,9¾)in/(23,24,25cm) from beg. Bind off.

■ **Pockets** Make 2 alike. Using **A** cast on 19 (19-21) sts and work in st st for 4(4,4¾)in/(10,10,12cm), ending with a p row then work in rib.
■ *1st row* P 1, * k 1, p 1; rep from * to end.
■ *2nd row* K 1, * p 1, k 1; rep from * to end. Rep 1st and 2nd rows once then 1st row again. Bind off loosely in rib.

■ **Buttonhole Loops** Make 8 alike. Cast on 3 sts using **A** and work in st st for 5cm (2in). Bind off.

■ **Finishing** Join shoulder seams. On each side edge mark a point 7½(7⅞,8½)in/(19,20,21.5cm) down from shoulder seam for armholes; sew bound-off edge of sleeves between markers. Join side and sleeve seams. Slip st pockets to fronts. Fold cast-on edge of hood in half and sew forming upper seam. Sew lower edges to neck edges easing in fullness. The buttonhole loops are sewn on later.

SECOND SECTION

■ **Back** using **B** cast on 67 (73-79) sts and work 4 rows in st st then work patt from chart, joining on **C**.
■ *1st row* K 5 (0-3) **B**, * 1 **C**, 7 **B**; * rep from * to * ending 1 **C**, 5 (0-3) **B**. Mark on chart the position where row begins and ends according to size. Cont working from chart until the zigzag is completed on 8th row, taking great care not to pull the yarn tightly on wrong side.
■ Work next 5 rows in **B**; the spots will be embroidered afterwards. Work rem 8 rows of chart then cont in **B** only until work measures 17¼(18⅞,20½)in/(44,48,52)cm, from beg, ending with a p row. Work the 21 rows of patt as before then cont in **B** until work measures 21¼(22¾,24½)in/(54,58,62cm) from beg. Work shoulder shaping as for Section 1.

■ **Left Front** Using **B** cast on 35 (38-41) sts and work 4 rows in st st then work patt from chart.
■ *1st row* K 5 (0-3) **B**, * 1 **C**, 7 **B**; * rep from * to * 2 (2-3) times more, 1 **C**, 5 **B**. Cont in patt as now set until 21st row has been worked then cont in **B** only until work measures 17¼(18⅞,20½)in/(44,48,52cm) from beg, ending with a p row. Work patt as before and *at same time*, when work measures 19¾(20¾,22⅜)in/(50,53,57cm), from beg, ending with a k row work neck and shoulder shaping as for Section 1, changing to **B** after patt is completed.

■ **Right Front** Work as for left front reversing arrangement of patt and all shapings.

■ **Sleeves** Using **B** cast on 45 (49-53) sts and work 4 rows in st st then work patt from chart.
■ *1st row* K 2 (4-6) **B**, * 1 **C**, 7 **B**; * rep from * to * ending 1 **C**, 2 (4-6) **B**. Cont working from chart but shape sides of sleeve as for Section 1, working 1st inc at each side on 6th row of patt. When the 21 rows have been worked complete as for Section 1 using **B** only.

■ **Hood** Using **B** cast on 61 (65-69) sts and work 4 rows in st st. Now begin working patt from chart arranging it as for sleeves; when

the 21st row has been worked, cont in **B** only and complete as for Section 1.

■ **Buttonhole Loops** Make these as for Section 1 but using **B**.

■ **Finishing** Follow instructions given for Section 1 apart from pockets. Swiss darn spots in **C** and **A** on back and fronts, leaving 4 or more rows at top before start of zigzag. Embroider spots on

sleeves and hood. Slip one section inside the other with p sides tog. Neatly slip-st sections tog all along front and lower edges, around front edge of hood and lower edges of sleeves. Fold buttonhole loops in half and sew to fronts of each section placing top one just below neck and rem 3 on each front spaced about 3¾(4,4⅛)in/(9.5,10,10.5cm), apart. Sew 4 buttons to match the loops.

SCARF, ROLL COLLAR HOOD WITH VISOR, LEGWARMERS AND CHILD'S MITTENS

CHECKLIST

Materials
Scarf *Laine Plassard* Florès: 4 balls of No 9, yellow. Pair of needles size 8.

Roll Collar *Bouton d'Or 100 per cent* Mohair Gratté: *2 balls of Prunelle, pink. pair each of needles size 8 and 10.*

Hood with Visor *Ann Blatt Soft'Anny* Kid Mohair: *2 balls of No 1349, blue. Pair each of needles size 7 and 5.*

Leg-warmers *Bouton d'Or 11 per cent* Mohair Gratté: *2 balls of Prunelle, pink* (**A**), *and 1 ball of Anemone* (**B**). *Pair of 8 needles.*

Child's Mittens *Berger du Nord* Kid Mohair: *1 ball of No 8246, coral. Pair each of needles size 2 and 5.*

Sizes
Scarf, roll collar hood with visor and leg-warmers are adult sized, and can easily be adjusted to be larger or smaller. Mittens are in two sizes, to fit ages 6 (8) years.

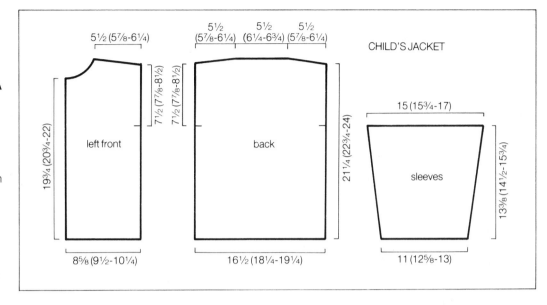

CHILD'S JACKET

left front · back · sleeves

5½ (5⅞-6¼)

5½ (5⅞-6¼) · 5½ (6¼-6¾) · 5½ (5⅞-6¼)

7½ (7⅞-8½)

7½ (7⅞-8½)

19¾ (20¾-22)

21¼ (22¾-24)

15 (15¾-17)

13⅜ (14½-15¾)

8⅝ (9½-10¼)

16½ (18¼-19¼)

11 (12⅝-13)

INSTRUCTIONS

▦ **Scarf** Cast on 35 sts and work in rib.

▦ *1st row* (right side) K 2, * p 1, k 1; rep from * to last st, k 1.

▦ *2nd row* K 1, * p 1, k 1; rep from * to end. Rep these 2 rows until work measures 82½in (210cm) from beg. Bind off in rib.

▦ **Roll Collar** Using smaller needles, cast on 90 sts and work in k 2, p 2 rib.

▦ *1st row* (right side) K 2, * p 2, k 2; rep from * to end.

▦ *2nd row* P 2, * k 2, p 2 *; rep from * to end. Rep these 2 rows until work measures 4¾in (12cm) from beg then change to larger needles and cont in same rib but inc 1 st at both ends every other row until work measures 11¾in (30cm) from beg. Bind off loosely in rib. Join side edges with a neat

backstitch seam.

▦ **Hood with Visor** Beg at lower edge cast on 104 sts using smaller needles and work in k 1, p 1 rib for 3½in (9cm).

▦ *Dec row* Rib 5, [p 2 tog, rib 2] 24 times, rib 3. Cont on rem 80 sts; change to larger needles and beg with a k row work in st st. Cont until work measures 7½in (19cm) from beg, ending with a p row.

▦ **Front Opening** *1st row* K 34 and leave these sts on a spare needle, bind off next 12 sts, k to end. Cont on 34 sts now rem on needle and p 1 row. ** Bind off 3 sts at beg of next row, 2 sts at same edge on next alt row and 1 st on next 3 alt rows then dec 1 st at same edge on foll 4th row. Cont on rem 25 sts until work measures 11¾in (30cm) from beg, ending at opening after a p row. ** Cut yarn and with wrong side facing rejoin

to first group of sts. Cont in same way from ** to ** but ending at side edge after a p row.

▦ *Next row* K 25, turn, cast on 30 sts, turn, then k across other group of 25 sts. Cont on these 80 sts in st st until work measures 13¾in (35cm) from beg, ending with a p row then shape top.

▦ *1st row* K 3, [k 2 tog, SKPO, k 6] 7 times, k 2 tog, SKPO, k 3. Work 5 rows on rem 64 sts.

▦ *7th row* K 2, [k 2 tog, SKPO, k 4] 7 times, k 2 tog, SKPO, k 2. Work 5 rows on rem 48 sts.

▦ *13th row* K 1, [k 2 tog, SKPO, k 2] 7 times, k 2 tog, SKPO, k 1. Work 3 rows on rem 32 sts.

▦ *17th row* [K 2 tog] 16 times. Cut yarn, thread end through rem 16 sts, draw up tightly and sew securely then join back seam of hood.

▦ **Visor** With right side of work

facing and using larger needles, pick up and k 32 sts along cast-on edge at top of front opening. Shape by working shortened rows as foll:

▦ *1st row* (wrong side) P 22, turn.

▦ *2nd row* K 12, turn; there are 10 sts left unworked at each side.

▦ *3rd row* P 16, turn.

▦ *4th row* K 20, turn.

▦ *5th row* P 23, turn.

▦ *6th row* K 26, turn.

▦ *7th row* P 29, turn.

▦ *8th row* K all the 32 sts. Now k 1 row on wrong side to form a ridge for foldline. Cont in st st beg with another k row and bind off 3 sts at beg of next 4 rows and 4 sts at beg of next 2 rows. Bind off rem 12 sts.

▦ **Front Border** With right side of work facing and using smaller needles, pick up and k 54 sts around rem edges of opening, beg and ending next to visor. Work 2 rows in g st. Sew ends of this border at sides of visor; fold last part of visor to inside along fold-line and slip-st bound-off edges in place.

▦ **Leg-warmers** Beg at lower edge cast on 60 sts using **A** and work in k 1, p 1 rib. Cont until work measures 7⅞in (20cm) from beg then work 4 rows in **B**, 6 rows in **A**, 4 rows in **B**, 4 rows in **A**. Bind off in rib. Make another leg-warmer in same way. Join back seams.

▦ **Child's Mitts** *Both mitts alike* With smaller needles cast on 26 (30) sts and work in k 1, p 1 rib for 1½in (4cm). Change to larger needles and beg with a k row work in st st. Work 2 rows then shape for thumb.

▦ *3rd row* K 12 (14), pick up loop lying between needles and k it through the back = k loop, k 2, k loop, k 12 (14). Work 3 rows.

▦ *7th row* K 12 (14), k loop, k 4, k loop, k 12 (14). Cont to inc in these positions on every foll 4th row once (twice) more. P 1 row on 32 (38) sts.

▦ **Thumb** K 12 (14) and leave these sts on a holder, k next 8 (10) sts, turn leaving rem 12 (14) sts on another holder. Cast on 1 st at beg of next 2 rows then cont on 10 (12) sts until thumb measures 1 (1⅛)in/ (2.5,3cm), from beg. On foll row, k 2 sts tog all along row, cut yarn, pass end through rem sts, draw up tightly and sew securely. Join thumb seam. With right side facing and using larger needles, pick up and k 2 sts at base of thumb, k rem 12 (14) sts left on second holder.

▦ *Next row* P 14 (16), then p sts from first holder. Cont on 26 (30) sts until work measures 5⅛(5⅞)in/(13,15cm), from beg, ending with a p row then shape top.

▦ *1st row* K 1, SKPO, k 7 (9), k 2 tog, k 2, SKPO, k 7 (9), k 2 tog, k 1. P 1 row.

▦ *3rd row* K 1, SKPO, k 5 (7), k 2 tog, k 2, SKPO, k 5 (7), k 2 tog, k 1. Cont to dec in same positions every other row 2(3) times.

▦ Cut yarn, pass end through rem sts, draw up tightly and sew securely then join seam along side of hand.

NEGATIVE / POSITIVE

Black plays white and both unite to form a winning team when father and son wear these striking sweaters together. The sweaters are knitted in stockinette stitch, and are designed to complement each other. To make it easier to pull on, the youngster's version is buttoned at the shoulder, and the smaller of the adult sizes would fit an average sized woman – so if you can't beat them, join them! The instructions given are for hand knitting, but the sweaters can also be machine knitted, following the charts.

CHECKLIST

Materials
Adult's version *Chat Botté* Nénuphar: *9 (10) balls of black* (**B**), *and 8 balls of white* (**W**). *Pair each of needles size 2 and 3; set of four double-pointed needles size 2.*

Child's version *Chat Botté* Nénuphar: *4 (5) balls of black* (**B**), *and 3 balls of white* (**W**). *Pair each of needles size 2 and 3; 5 small black buttons.*

Sizes
Adult's version, two sizes, to fit 34/36 (42/44)in, 82/92 (102/107)cm, chest.
Child's version, two sizes, to fit ages 6 (8) years.
Actual measurements shown on the diagrams.

Stitches used
K 2, p 2 rib; patt, worked from charts. Take care to wind yarns around each other when changing color.

Gauge
Using larger needles and working in patt, 33 sts and 39 rows to 4in (10cm). Work a sample on 48 sts.

Note *This design can be worked on a Knitmaster 600 or 700 knitting machine. Tension 7 for the patt. Tension 3 for the ribbing. For hand knitting the row tension will be looser and we therefore advise you to work only one row between each band of patt on the adult version only, indicated at side of chart thus:* 1.

INSTRUCTIONS

ADULT'S VERSION

▦ **Back** With smaller needles and **B**, cast on 182 (198) sts.
▦ *1st row* (right side) P 2, * k 2, p 2, rep from * to end.
▦ *2nd row* K 2, * p 2, k 2, rep from * to end. Rep these 2 rows for 2(3⅛)in/5,8cm), ending with 2nd row.
▦ With larger needles work 4(8) rows st st with **B**. Foll chart reading k rows right to left as foll:
▦ *For 1st size, 1st row* ∗ K 4 **B**, 4

W, 5 **B**, 3 **W**, 4 **B**, 4 **W**; rep from ∗ to last 14 sts, k 4 **B**, 4 **W**, 5 **B**, 1 **W**.
▦ *2nd row* P 1 **W**, 1 **B**, 1 **W**, 4 **B**, 4 **W**, 3 **B**, ∗ p 1 **B**, 4 **W**, 4 **B**, 2 **W**, 1 **B**, 1 **W**, 4 **B**, 4 **W**, 3 **B**, rep from ∗ to end.
▦ *For 2nd size, 1st row* ∗ K 4 **B**, 4 **W**, 5 **B**, 3 **W**, 4 **B**, 4 **W**, rep from ∗ to last 6 sts, k 4 **B**, 2 **W**.
▦ *2nd row* P 3 **W**, 3 **B**, ∗ p 1 **B**, 4 **W**, 4 **B**, 2 **W**, 1 **B**, 1 **W**, 4 **B**, 4 **W**, 3 **B**, rep from ∗ to end.
▦ Cont working from chart as now set until work measures 28(29½)in/(71,75cm) from beg. Bind off.

▦ **Front** Work as for the back until work measures 25¼(26¾)in/ (64,68cm) from beg, ending with a p row.

▦ **Neck Shaping** *Next row* Patt 66 (72) sts and leave these sts of left front on a spare needle, bind off next 50 (54) sts, then patt to end. Cont on 66 (72) sts rem on needle for right front as foll: patt 1 row. ∗∗ Bind off 4 sts at beg of next row, 3 sts at same edge every other row once, 2 sts every other row 1(2) times, and 1 st every other row 3

times. Work without further shaping until front is 28(29½)in/ (71,75cm) from beg. Bind off rem sts for shoulder edge. ∗∗.
▦ Rejoin yarn to neck edge of left front sts and keeping patt correct cont as for right front from ∗∗ to ∗∗.

▦ **Sleeves** With smaller needles and **B**, cast on 106 (110) sts and work 3(4)in/(8,10cm) k 2, p 2 rib as for back, ending with a 2nd row. With larger needles work 1 (5) rows st st with **B**.
▦ Foll chart for sleeve reading p

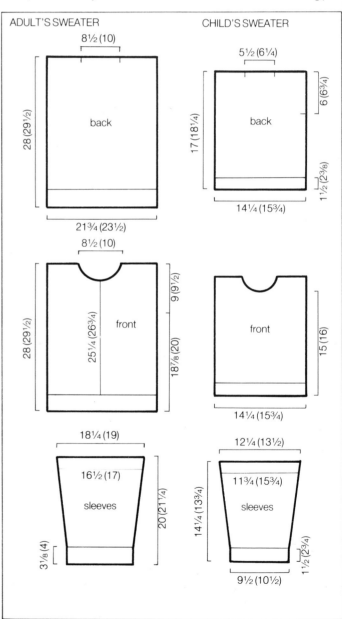

ADULT'S SWEATER

8½ (10)

28 (29½)

back

21¾ (23½)

8½ (10)

28 (29½) · 25¼ (26¾) · 18⅞ (20)

front

9 (9½)

18¼ (19)

16½ (17)

sleeves

3⅛ (4) · 20 (21¼)

CHILD'S SWEATER

5½ (6¼)

6 (6¾)

17 (18¼)

back

1½ (2⅜)

14¼ (15¾)

front

15 (16)

14¼ (15¾)

12¼ (13½)

11¾ (15¾)

sleeves

1½ (2¾)

9½ (10½)

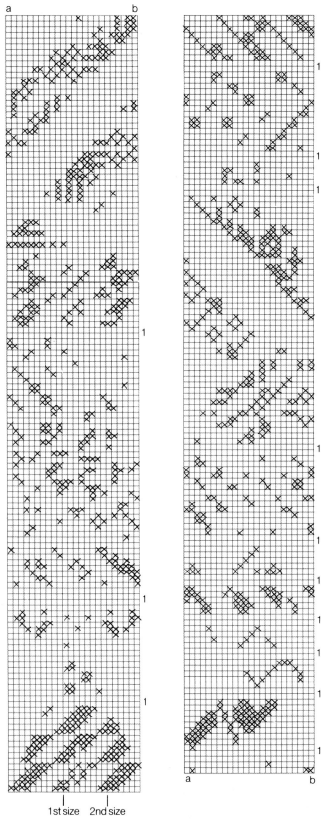

1st size   2nd size

charts for back

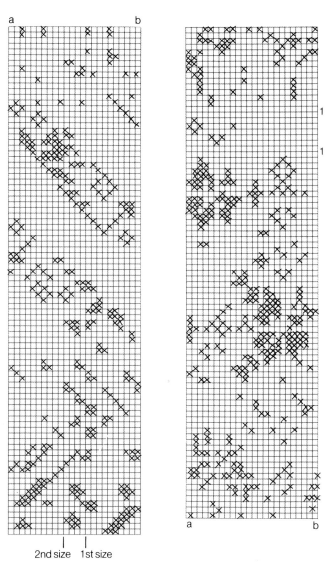

2nd size   1st size

charts for sleeves

rows from left to right as foll:

▣ *For 1st size, 1st row* P with **B**.

▣ *2nd row* K 4 **B**, 3 **W**, 17 **B**, rep from * to last 10 sts, k 4 **B**, 3 **W**, 3 **B**.

▣ *3rd row* P 4 **B**, 3 **W**, 3 **B**, * p 1 **B**, 3 **W**, 7 **B**, 2 **W**, 5 **B**, 3 **W**, 3 **B**, rep from * to end.

▣ *For 2nd size, 1st row* P with **B**.

▣ *2nd row* * K 4 **B**, 3 **W**, 17 **B**, rep from * to last 14 sts, k 4 **B**, 3 **W**, 7 **B**.

▣ *3rd row* P 1 **B**, 2 **W**, 5 **B**, 3 **W**, 3 **B**, * p 1 **B**, 3 **W**, 7 **B**, 2 **W**, 5 **B**, 3 **W**, 3 **B**, rep from * to end.

▣ Cont working from chart as now set but inc 1 st at both ends of every 8th row 16 times. Work

without further shaping until sleeve measures 19⅛(20⅜)in/ (48.5,51.5cm), ending with a wrong-side row. Work 4 rows g st with **B**. Bind off loosely.

▣ **Finishing** Join the back and front shoulder seams. With right side of work facing and using three double-pointed needles and **B**, pick up k 114 (118) sts around front neck edge and 74 (78) sts across back neck. With the 4th needle work in rounds of k 2, p 2 rib for 1½in (4cm). Bind off loosely in rib. Join side seams for 18⅞(20)in/(48,51cm). Join the sleeve seams. Sew in the sleeves.

CHILD'S VERSION

Back With smaller needles and **B**, cast on 120 (132) sts and work in k 1, p 1 rib for 1½(2⅜)in/ (4,6cm). With larger needles work 4 (8) rows st st with **W**. Foll chart, reading k rows from right to left as foll:

1st size, 1st row * K 2 **W**, 2 **B**, 4 **W**, 3 **B**, 5 **W**, 4 **B**, 4 **W**, rep from * to end.

2nd row P 3 **W**, 4 **B**, 4 **W**, 1 **B**, 1 **W**, 2 **B**, 4 **W**, 3 **B**, 2 **W**, rep from * to end.

2nd size, 1st row * K 2 **W**, 2 **B**, 4 **W**, 3 **B**, 5 **W**, 4 **B**, 4 **W**, rep from * to last 12 sts, 2 **W**, 2 **B**, 4 **W**, 3 **B**, 1 **W**.

2nd row P 1 **W**, 2 **B**, 4 **W**, 3 **B**, 2 **W**, * p 3 **W**, 4 **B**, 4 **B**, 1 **W**, 1 **B**, 2 **W**, 4 **B**, 3 **W**, 2 **B**, rep from * to end.

Cont working from chart as now set until work measures 17(18¼)in/ (43,46cm) from beg. Bind off.

Front Work as for back until work measures 15(16⅛)in/ (38,41cm), from beg, ending with p row.

Neck Shaping *Next row* Patt 49 (52) sts, turn and leave rem sts on a spare needle.

** Bind off 4 sts at beg of next row, 3 sts at same edge every other row once, then 2 sts every other row and 1 st every other row 3 times. Work without further shaping until front measures 17(18⅛)in/(43,46cm), from beg. **

Using **W**, work buttonholes thus: k 6, bind off 2 sts, * k until there are 7 (8) sts on right-hand needle after the bound-off sts, bind off 2 sts, rep from * twice more, k to end.

K 1 more row with **W**, casting on 2 sts to complete each buttonhole. K 2 rows. Bind off.

With right side of work facing, rejoin yarn to sts on spare needle, bind off next 22 (28) sts, patt to end. Keeping patt correct work 1 row. Work as for left side from ** to **. Bind off.

Sleeves With smaller needles and **B**, cast on 80 (90) sts and work in k 1, p 1 rib for 1½(2¾)in/ (4,7cm).

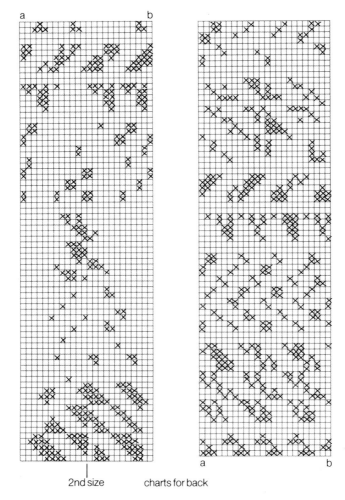

2nd size   charts for back

Using larger needles work 4 (8) rows st st with **W**. Foll chart for sleeve reading k rows from right to left as foll:

For 1st size, 1st row * K 3 **W**, 3 **B**, 1 **W**, 5 **B**, 1 **W**, 1 **B**, 1 **W**, 3 **B**, 1 **W**, 1 **B**, 1 **W**, 3 **B**, rep from * to last 8 sts, k 3 **W**, 3 **B**, 1 **W**, 1 **B**.

2nd row P 1 **B**, 1 **W**, 3 **B**, 3 **W**, * p 3 **B**, 1 **W**, 1 **B**, 1 **W**, 3 **B**, 1 **W**, 1 **B**, 1 **W**, 5 **B**, 1 **W**, 3 **B**, 3 **W**, rep from * to end.

For 2nd size, 1st row * K 3 **W**, 3 **B**, 1 **W**, 5 **B**, 1 **W**, 1 **B**, 1 **W**, 3 **B**, 1 **W**, 1 **B**, 1 **W**, 3 **B**, rep from * to last 18 sts, 3 **W**, 3 **B**, 1 **W**, 5 **B**, 1 **W**, 1 **B**, 1 **W**, 3 **B**.

2nd row P 3 **B**, 1 **W**, 1 **B**, 1 **W**, 5 **B**, 1 **W**, 3 **B**, 3 **W**, * p 3 **B**, 1 **W**, 1 **B**, 1 **W**, 3 **B**, 1 **W**, 1 **B**, 1 **W**, 5 **B**, 1 **W**, 3 **B**, 3 **W**. Cont working from chart as set but inc 1 st at both ends of every 10th row 10 times. Work without further shaping until sleeve measures 13¼(14⅞)in/ (33.5,37.5cm) from beg, ending

with a wrong-side row. Work 4 rows g st with **B**. Bind off.

Finishing Join right shoulder seam. With right side of work facing and using the smaller needles pick up and k 60 (64) sts around front neck edge and 45 (51) sts across back neck.

1st row P 1, * k 1, p 1, rep from * to end.

2nd row K 1, * p 1, k 1, rep from * to end. Rep these 2 rows for 2cm (¾in), ending at left front shoulder.

Next row Rib 2, bind off 2 sts, rib to end.

Next row Rib to last 2 sts, cast on 2 sts, rib to end. Cont in rib until the neck band measures 1in (2.5cm). Bind off loosely in rib.

Join the side seams for 10¾(11⅜)in/(27.5,29cm), leaving the remainder free for the armholes.

Join the sleeve seams and sew them in position. Sew on buttons.

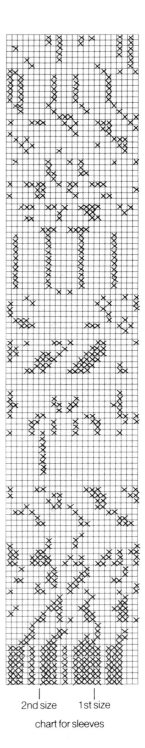

2nd size   1st size

chart for sleeves

KEY

□ = black
⊠ = white

ANIMAL MAGIC

Children adore dressing up and have a natural love of animals, so they will instantly feel part of the animal kingdom when they wear these charming and imaginative sweaters, with their animal faces and matching hoods. The crafty fox and the gentle lamb, the mischievous mouse and the clever cat – for once they can all live together in harmony in a happy world of make-believe. All the designs are easy and quick to knit, using only simple stitches.

CHECKLIST

Materials

Fox *La Droguerie* Mohair: *180(190-200)g of rust (**A**), and 25(30-35)g of white (**B**). Small amount of 4-ply yarn in black for nose. Pair each of needles size 5 and 8; 2 buttons to fasten; 4 buttons for eyes.*

Lamb *La Droguerie* Igloo: *290(310-330)g of white (**A**), and 20g of peach (**B**). Pair each of needles size 10 and 11; 2 buttons to fasten; 4 buttons for eyes; yarn for embroidery.*

Mouse *La Droguerie* Mohair: *150(160-170)g of pink (**A**). La Droguerie Angora: 45(50-55)g of gray (**B**). Pair each of needles size 5 and 8; 2 buttons to fasten; 4 buttons for eyes; russia braid for whiskers; scrap of dress stiffening for teeth; yarn for embroidery.*

Cat *La Droguerie* Mohair: *90(100-110)g of gray (**A**), and 100(110-120)g of white (**B**). Pair each of needles size 5 and 8; 2 buttons to fasten; 4 buttons for eyes; russia braid for whiskers; pink yarn for embroidering nose.*

Sizes

Sweaters each have the same shape and are in three sizes, to fit ages 2 (4-6) years. Actual measurements shown on diagram.
Hoods are in one size, to fit a child of about 4 to 6 years. The hoods vary slightly in shape and are shown on separate diagrams.

Stitches used

Single rib; g st; st st.

Gauge

Over g st using size 8 needles and Mohair, 15 sts and 28 rows to 4in (10cm). Work a sample on 13 sts.
Over st st using size 8 needles and Mohair, 15 sts and 22 rows to 4in (10cm). Work a sample on 20 sts.
Over g st using size 11 needles and Igloo, 9 sts and 14 rows to 4in (10cm). Work a sample on 13 sts.

INSTRUCTIONS

FOX

▦ **Sweater Back** With smaller needles and **A** cast on 47 (49-53) sts and work in rib.
▦ ** *1st row* (right side) P 1, * k 1, p 1; rep from * to end.
▦ *2nd row* K 1, * p 1, k 1; rep from * to end. Rep these 2 rows until work measures 1½in (4cm) from beg, ending with a 2nd rib row (but for 2nd size inc 1 st in center of last row). **.
▦ Change to larger needles and cont on 47 (50-53) sts working in g st. Cont until work measures 7⅛(7⅞,8⅝)in/(18,20,22cm) from beg.

28

Armhole Shaping Bind off 4 sts at beg of next 2 rows then cont on rem 39 (42-45) sts until work measures 13(14⅛,15⅜)in/(33, 36,39cm) from beg. Bind off all sts for shoulders and back neck.

Front Work as for back until work measures 10¼(11⅜, 12⅝)in/(26,29,32cm) from beg, ending with a wrong-side row.

Neck Shaping *1st row* K 17 (18-19) and leave these sts of left front on a spare needle, bind off next 5 (6-7) sts, k to end. Cont on 17 (18-19) sts now rem on needle for right front. *** Dec 1 st at neck edge on next 4 rows then at same edge on next 3 alt rows. Cont on rem 10 (11-12) sts until work matches back to shoulder edge. Bind off. Rejoin yarn to neck edge of left front sts and complete as for right front from *** to end reversing shapings.

Sleeves With smaller needles and **A** cast on 31 (33-37) sts and work as for back ribbing from ** to **. 31 (34-37) sts. Change to larger needles and work in g st but inc 1 st at both ends of every foll 6th (6th-7th) row 8 times. Cont on 47 (50-53) sts until work measures 10¼(11,11¾)in/(26,28,30cm) from beg. Bind off.

Finishing and Neck Border On bound-off edge of back mark center 19 (20-21) sts which will form neckline, leaving 10 (11-12) sts each side for shoulders. Join right shoulder seam. With right side of work facing and using smaller needles and **A**, pick up and k 41 (43-45) sts around front neck edge and 24 (24-26) sts across back neck. 65 (69-71) sts. Beg with 2nd row work 6 rows in k 1, p 1 rib then bind off in rib. Join right shoulder seam for the first 3 (4-5) sts from side edges. Along rem edge of front work 2 buttonhole loops, one near to neck edge and the other half-way along. Sew buttons to back shoulder to correspond. Sew bound-off edge of sleeves to sides of armholes and sew armhole binding-off to a corresponding depth on sides of sleeves. Join side and sleeve seams.

■ **Pocket** With larger needles and **A** cast on 3 sts for lower point; the nose is worked later. Work in st st but inc 1 st at both ends of 3rd row, work 4 rows straight, inc 1 st at both ends of next row and next 3 (4-5) alt rows. Cont on 13 (15-17) sts until work measures 4(4¼,4¼)in/(10,11,11cm) from beg. Bind off.

■ For nose use the black 4-ply yarn double; cast on 3 sts using larger needles and work in st st. Inc 1 st at both ends of 2nd row then work 3 rows straight. Bind off. With p side of nose to k side of pocket slip-st nose to lower point.

■ With right side of work facing and using larger needles and **B**, pick up and k 15 (17-17) sts along one side edge of pocket. Rep 2nd rib row then keeping rib correct

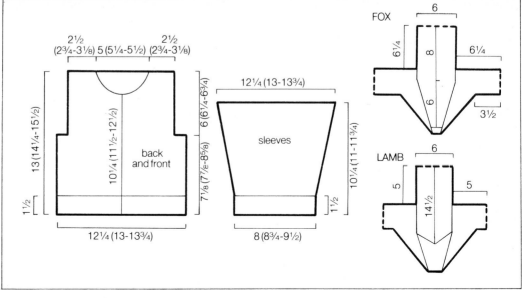

FOX

LAMB

dec 1 st at lower edge of next 3 rows. Bind off in rib. Work similar border along other side edge.

◫ **Ears** For outer section cast on 3 sts using larger needles and **A**. Work in rib but inc 1 st at both ends of every other row 4 times then work 4 rows straight. Bind off in rib.

◫ For inner section cast on 3 sts using larger needles and **B** work in rib, inc 1 st at both ends of every alt row 3 times then work 4 rows straight. Bind off in rib. Placing bound-off edges level sew outer and inner sections tog neatly. Sew ears to top of pocket and sew on eyes. Sew pocket to center front just above ribbing.

◫ **Hood** For center section cast on 3 sts using larger needles and **A**. Work in st st but inc 1 st at both ends of 2nd row, work 4 rows straight then inc 1 st at both ends of next row, then every foll 3rd row 8 times more. Cont on these 23 sts and work 7⅞in (20cm) without shaping, ending with a p row. Cut yarn and leave sts on a holder. Work nose as for pocket but after the inc row work 4 rows straight then bind off these 5 sts.

◫ Sew nose to lower point of hood in same way as for pocket. On left side edge of center section mark off the first 7½in (19cm). With right side of work facing and using larger needles and **A**, pick up and k 39 sts on marked section. Rep 2nd rib row then keeping rib correct dec 1 st at lower edge on next 20 rows. Cont on rem 19 sts until work measures 6¼in (16cm) measured along straight side edge, ending with a wrong-side row. Cut yarn and leave sts on a holder.

◫ Work similar border along right side edge of center section, reversing shapings; when work is same length as first side, ending with a wrong-side row, cont as foll. Work in rib across 19 sts of this side section, cont in rib across 23 sts of center section then rib sts of first side section. 61 sts. Change to **A** and cont in rib across all sts for 3in (9cm). Bind off in rib.

◫ **Ears** For outer section cast on

3 sts using larger needles and **A**. Work in rib but inc 1 st at both ends of every other row 6 times. Work 2 rows on these 15 sts then bind off in rib.

◫ For inner section cast on 3 sts using larger needles and **B**. Work in rib but inc 1 st at both ends of every other row 5 times. Work 1 row on these 13 sts then bind off in rib. Placing bound-off edges level sew inner section to outer section with neat sts.

◫ **Finishing** Join back seams of hood and make a neat backstitch seam at center front. Sew ears to top of hood. Sew on buttons for eyes.

LAMB

◫ **Sweater Back** With smaller needles and **A** cast on 29 (31-33) sts and work in rib as for Fox; cont until work measures 1½in (4cm) from beg, ending with a 2nd rib row. Change to larger needles and work in g st. Cont until work measures 7⅛(7⅞,8⅝)in/ (18,20,22cm) from beg.

◫ **Armhole Shaping** Bind off 3 sts at beg of next 2 rows then cont on rem 23 (25-27) sts until work measures 13(14⅛,15⅜)in/ (33,36,39cm) from beg. Bind off all sts for shoulder and back neck edges.

◫ **Front** Work as for back until you have worked 9 rows fewer than on back.

◫ **Neck Shaping** *1st row* K 10 (11-11) and leave these sts on a spare needle, bind off next 3 (3-5) sts, k to end. Cont on 10 (11-11) sts now rem on needle. Dec 1 st at neck edge on next 3 rows then at same edge on next alt row. Work 3 rows on rem 6 (7-7) sts then bind off these sts for shoulder edge. Rejoin yarn to neck edge of first group of sts and complete in same way, reversing neck shapings.

◫ **Sleeves** With smaller needles and **A** cast on 17 (19-21) sts and work in rib for 1½in (4cm) but inc 1 st in center of last row. 18 (20-22) sts. Change to larger needles and work in g st but inc 1 st at both ends of every foll 4th (4th-5th) row

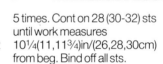

5 times. Cont on 28 (30-32) sts until work measures 10¼(11,11¾)in/(26,28,30cm) from beg. Bind off all sts.

◫ **Finishing and Neck Border** On bound-off edge of back mark center 11 (11-13) sts for neckline leaving 6 (7-7) sts on each side for shoulders. Join right shoulder seam. With right side of work facing and using smaller needles and **A**, pick up and k 28 (28-30) sts around front neck edge and 15 (15-17) sts across back neck. 43 (43-47) sts. Beg with 2nd row work 4 rows in rib then bind off in rib. Work remainder of sweater as for Fox.

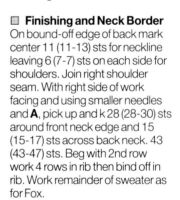

◫ **Pocket** With smaller needles and **B** cast on 5 (5-7) sts and work in st st. Inc 1 st at both ends of 2nd row then cont on 7 (7-9) sts until work measures 2⅜(2⅜,2¾)in/ (6,6,7cm) from beg, ending with a p row. Now form point in **A** at center.

◫ *1st row* K 3 (3-4) **B**, join on small ball of **A**, k 1 **A**, then 3 (3-4) **B**.

◫ *2nd row* P 2 (2-3) **B**, twist yarns, p 3 **A**, join on a small ball of **B**, p 2 (2-3) **B**. Always twisting yarns when changing color work 2 extra sts in **A** at center on next 2 (2-3) rows. Bind off all sts.

◫ **Ears** For outer section cast on 3 (3-5) sts using smaller needles

and **A**. Work in rib but inc 1 st at both ends of every other row twice then work 4 rows on these 7 (7-9) sts. Bind-off in rib. For inner section cast on 3 (3-5) sts using smaller needles and **B**. Work in rib but inc 1 st at both ends of every other row twice. Work 2 rows on these 7 (7-9) sts then bind off in rib.

◫ Placing bound-off edges level sew inner and outer sections neatly tog. Sew ears to top of pocket and sew on eyes.

◫ Embroider the nose with a deeper peach color. Sew the pocket to center front just above ribbing.

◫ **Hood** Tension for this, working in st st on smaller needles is 11 sts and 14 rows to 4in (10cm).

◫ For center section cast on 5 sts using smaller needles and **B**. Work in st st and inc 1 st at both ends of 3rd row, work 7 rows straight then inc 1 st at both ends of next row. 9 sts. Now begin forming point in **A** at center.

◫ *12th row* P 4 **B**, join on a ball of **A**, p 1 **A**, then p 4 **B**.

◫ *13th row* K 3 **B**, twist yarns, k 3 **A**, join on a small ball of **B**, k 3 **B**.

◫ *14th row* P 2 **B**, twist yarns, p 5 **A**, 2 **B**. Inc 1 st at both ends of next row, then every foll 4th row 3 times more but *at same time* cont to work 2 extra sts in **A** at center until all sts are in **A**. When incs are completed cont on these 17 sts and work 7⅛in (18cm) without shaping, ending with a p row. Cut yarn and leave sts on a holder.

On each side edge mark a point 7⅞in (18cm) from beg. With right side of work facing and using smaller needles and **A**, pick up and k 29 sts along this marked section on left side. Rep 2nd rib row then keeping rib correct dec 1 st at lower edge on next 18 rows. Cont on rem 11 sts until work measures 5⅛in (13cm) along straight side edge, ending with a wrong-side row. Cut yarn and leave sts on a holder. Work similar border along right side edge of center, reversing shapings. When it is the same length as first section ending with a wrong-side row cont as foll: work in rib across these 11 sts, cont in rib across 17 sts of center section then cont in rib across 11 sts of first side section. 39 sts. Cont across all sts in rib for 4in (10cm). Bind off in rib.

Ears For outer section cast on 5 sts using smaller needles and **A**; work in rib but inc 1 st at both ends of every other row 3 times then cont on 11 sts until work measures 5⅛in (13cm) from beg. Bind off in rib.

For inner section cast on 5 sts using smaller needles and **B**. Work in rib but inc 1 st at both ends of 3rd row then cont on these 7 sts until work measures 4¼in (11cm) from beg. Bind off in rib.

Finishing Placing bound-off edges level sew inner and outer sections of ears neatly tog. Join back seams of hood and join ribbed section with a neat backstitch join at center front. Sew ears to top of hood. Embroider nose with deeper peach shade. Sew on eyes.

MOUSE

Sweater For back, front and sleeves work as for sweater of Fox design but using **A** (pink).

Finishing and Neck Border As for Fox sweater.

Pocket With larger needles and **B** cast on 4 (5-6) sts and work in st st but inc 1 st at both ends of

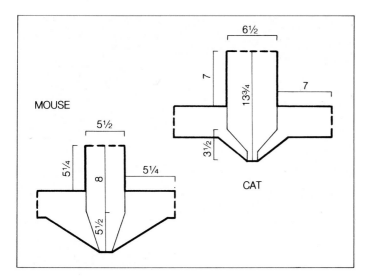

every other row 6 times. Cont on 16 (17-18) sts until work measures 3½(3½,4)in/(9,9,10cm) from beg. Bind off. With right side facing and using larger needles and **B**, pick up and k 15 (15-17) sts along one side edge of pocket. Rep 2nd rib row then keeping rib correct dec 1 st at lower edge on next 3 rows. Bind off in rib. Work similar border on other side.

■ **Ears** With larger needles and **B** cast on 3 (3-5) sts for outer section and work in rib. Inc 1 st at both ends of every other row 3 times then work 6 rows on these 9 (9-11) sts, bind off in rib. For inner section cast on 3 (3-5) sts using larger needles and **A**. Work in rib but inc 1 st at both ends of every alt row 3 times then work 3 rows on these 9 (9-11) sts. Bind off in rib.
■ Placing cast-on and bound-off edges level sew inner and outer sections neatly tog. Sew ears to top of pocket. Sew pocket to center front just above ribbing. Cut whiskers and pass through base of pocket. Cut out teeth from stiffened fabric and sew in place. Embroider nose in black yarn. Sew eyes in place.

■ **Hood** With larger needles and **B** cast on 3 sts for center section and work in st st; inc 1 st at both ends of every foll 3rd row 5 times then every foll 4th row 4 times. Cont on these 21 sts until work measures 13⅜in (34cm) from beg, ending with a p row. Cut yarn

and leave sts on a holder. On each side edge mark a point 8in (20.5cm) from beg. With right side of work facing and using larger needles and **B**, pick up and k 39 sts along this marked section on left side. Rep 2nd rib row then keeping rib correct dec 1 st at lower edge on next 20 rows. Cont on rem 19 sts until work measures 5¼in (13.5cm) from beg, ending with a wrong-side row. Cut yarn and leave sts on a holder.
■ Work other side section along right edge of center in same way, reversing shapings, and when this section measures same length ending with a wrong-side row cont as foll: work in rib across these 19 sts, cont in rib across 21 sts of center section then cont in rib across 19 sts of left side section. 59 sts. Cont in rib across all sts for 3½in (9cm) then bind off in rib.

■ **Ears** With larger needles and **B** cast on 5 sts for outer section and work in rib but inc 1 st at both ends of every other row 5 times. Cont on these 15 sts and work 6 rows straight then bind off in rib. For inner section cast on 5 sts using larger needles and **A**. Work in rib but inc 1 st at both ends of every alt row 4 times. Cont on these 13 sts and work 5 rows straight. Bind off in rib. Placing bound-off edges level sew inner and outer sections tog neatly. Sew back seams of hood and make a neat backstitch seam at center front. Sew ears to top of hood. Complete the

features as for the pocket.

CAT

■ **Sweater** For back and front work as for sweater of Fox design using **A** for ribbing then change to larger needles and, working in st st, work in stripes of 4 rows **B**, 4 rows **A**; complete as for Fox design.
■ **Sleeves** Work as for Fox sweater but after completing cuff change to larger needles and work in st st in stripes as for back and front; inc 1 st at both ends of every foll 6th row 2 (3-4) times then every foll 4th row 6 (5-4) times. Cont on 47 (50-53) sts until work measures 10¼(11,11¾)in/(26,28,30cm) from beg. Bind off.

■ **Pocket** With larger needles and **B** cast on 4 (5-6) sts and work in st st; work 2 rows straight then inc 1 st at both ends of next 10 rows. Cont on 24 (25-26) sts until work measures 3⅛(3⅛,3½)in/ (8,8,9cm) from beg. Bind off.
■ With right side of work facing and using larger needles and **B**, pick up and k 19 (19-21) sts along right side edge of center section. Rep 2nd rib row, then keeping rib correct shape both edges.
■ *1st row* Bind off 3, rib to last 8 sts, turn.
■ *2nd and even rows* Rib to end.
■ *3rd row* Bind off 2, rib to last 7 sts, turn.
■ *5th row* Bind off 2, rib to last 6 sts, turn. Cont to bind off 2 sts at beg of every other row and work 1 extra st before turning at end of same row 3 (3-4) times more. Work 1 row in rib on rem 6 sts then bind off in rib.
■ Work similar border along other side reversing shapings.

■ **Ears** With larger needles and **A** cast on 3 sts for outer section and work in rib but inc 1 st at both ends of every other row 3 times then cont on 9 sts for 6 rows. Bind off in rib. For inner section cast on 3 sts using larger needles and **B**; work in rib but inc 1 st at both ends of every alt row twice then cont on 7 sts for 5 rows. Bind off in rib. Holding bound-off edges level sew inner and outer sections tog

neatly. Sew ears to top of pocket and sew pocket to center front of sweater just above ribbing. Embroider nose in pink yarn. Cut whiskers and pass through base of pocket. Sew on eyes.

■ **Hood** For center section cast on 5 sts using larger needles and **B**. Beg with a k row work in st st for 9 rows then inc 1 st at both ends of next 5 rows. 15 sts. Now work in stripes of 4 rows **A**, 4 rows **B**; cont to inc 1 st at both ends of next 5 rows then cont on these 25 sts until work measures 13¾in (35cm) from beg, ending with a p row. Cut yarn and leave these sts on a holder.
■ On each side edge of this section mark a point 2⅜in (6cm) from beg. With right side of work facing and using larger needles and **B**, pick up and k 13 sts along right side edge on marked section. Rep 2nd rib row then keeping rib correct shape both edges. Bind off 2 sts at beg of next row and then every other row 5 times – these shapings are at lower edge – *and at same time* inc 1 st at opposite edge on every other row 5 times then cast on 15 sts at same edge on next alt row. 21 sts. Cont in rib without shaping for 7⅛in (18cm) ending with a wrong-side row.
■ Cut yarn and leave sts on a holder. Work other side section in same way reversing shapings. With right side facing and using larger needles and **B**, rib sts of first side section, then cont in rib across sts of center section then rib sts of second side section. Cont on these 67 sts and work in rib for 4in (10cm). Bind off in rib. Join side seams and make a neat back stitch seam at center front.

■ **Ears** For outer section cast on 3 sts using larger needles and **A**; work in rib but inc 1 st at both ends of every other row 4 times then work 6 rows straight. Bind off in rib. For inner section cast on 3 sts using larger needles and **B**; work in rib but inc 1 st at both ends of every other row 3 times. Work 5 rows straight then bind off in rib. Assemble ears as for pocket, sew to top of hood. Complete features as for pocket.

GYM TONIC

From head to toe, these girls are ideally equipped to carry out all the movements and execute all the steps that their teacher asks of them. The set includes long and short sleeved sweaters, leg-warmers, shorts and a bandeau – all needed to keep the muscles warm and help to prevent chills and cramps when they stop exercising. Knitted in bright, zingy colors, all the items are simple and quick to make – in fact they are so easy that the girls could knit their own accessories – it might give them a taste for the craft!

CHECKLIST

Materials
La Droguerie Fluo: 450 (450-500)g for long-sleeved sweater; 300 (300-350)g for short-sleeved sweater; 150 (150-200)g for tank-top; 200g for leg-warmers, using either one color or two or more colors; 150 g for shorts, and about 20g for bandeau. Pair each of needles sized 8 and 10.

Sizes
Three sizes, to fit ages 10 (12-14) years. Actual measurements shown on diagrams.

Stitches used
Single rib; double rib; st st; g st.

Gauge
For long and short-sleeved sweaters: over st st and using larger needles; 14 sts and 19 rows to 4in (10cm). Work a sample on 18 sts.
For tank top: working in g st and using larger needles; 14 sts and 27 rows to 4in (10cm). Work a sample on 18 sts.
For shorts and leg-warmers: working in k 2, p 2 rib and using larger needles; 15sts and 19 rows to 4in (10cm), flattening work when measuring. Work a sample on 22 sts.

INSTRUCTIONS

LONG-SLEEVED SWEATER

▦ **Back** With larger needles, cast on 55 (58-61) sts and work in st st. Cont until work measures 20¾(22,23¼)in/(53,56,59cm) from beg. Bind off loosely.

▦ **Front** Work exactly as for back.

▦ **Sleeves** With larger needles, cast on 33 (36-39) sts and work in st st but inc 1 st at both ends of every foll 10th row 2 (4-6) times then every foll 8th row 5 (3-1) times. Cont on 47 (50-53) sts until work measures 15(16⅛,17¼)in/(38,41,44cm) from beg. Bind off all sts.

▦ **Finishing** Join shoulder seams for 3½(4,4¼)in/(9,10,11cm) from each side edge leaving center section open for neckline. On each side edge place markers at a point 6½(7-7½)in/(16.5,17.5,19cm) down from shoulder seams for armholes and then sew bound-off edge of sleeves between the markers. Join side and sleeve seams.

SHORT-SLEEVED SWEATER

▦ **Back** With larger needles, cast on 49(52-55) sts and work in st st. Cont until work measures 15¾(17,18)in/(40,43,46cm) from beg, ending with a p row.

▦ **Neck Shaping** *1st row* K 18 (19-20) and leave these sts for

right back, bind off next 13 (14-15) sts, k to end. Cont on 18 (19-20) sts now rem on needle for left back and work 1 row. Bind off 3 sts at beg of next row and dec 1 st at neck edge on foll row. Bind off rem 14 (15-16) sts for shoulder edge. Rejoin yarn to neck edge of right back sts, bind off 3, p to end. Dec 1 st at neck edge on foll row, work 1 row on rem 14 (15-16) sts then bind off.

■ **Front** Work as for back until work measures 14½(15¾,17)in/ (37,40,43cm) from beg, ending with a p row.

■ **Neck Shaping** *1st row* K 19 (20-21) and leave these sts of left front on a spare needle, bind off next 11 (12-13) sts, k to end. Cont on 19 (20-21) sts now rem on needle for right front. ** Dec 1 st at neck edge on next 3 rows then dec 1 st at same edge every other row twice. Cont on rem 14 (15-16) sts until work matches back to shoulder edge. Bind off. Rejoin yarn to neck edge of left front sts and complete as for right front from ** to end, reversing shapings.

■ **Sleeves** With larger needles,

cast on 53 (56-59) sts and work in st st for 5⅞(6¼,6¾)in/ (15,16,17cm). Bind off all sts.

■ **Finishing** Join shoulder seams. On each side edge mark a point 7½(7⅞,8¼)in/ (19,20,21cm) down from shoulder seams for armholes and sew bound-off edge of sleeves between markers. Join side and sleeve seams.

TANK TOP

■ **Back** With larger needles cast on 61 (64-67) sts and work in g st.

Cont until work measures 5½(5⅞,6¼)in/(14,15,16cm) from beg, ending with a p row.

■ **Armhole Shaping** Bind off 4 sts at beg of next 2 rows, 3 sts at beg of next 2 rows, 2 sts at beg of next 4 rows and 1 st at beg of next 4 (6-8) rows. 35 (36-37) sts.

■ **Neck Shaping** *1st row* K 14 and leave these sts of right back on a spare needle, bind off next 7 (8-9) sts, k to end. Cont on 14 sts now rem on needle for left back and work 1 row. ** Bind off 2 sts at beg of next row and every other row twice and then 1 st 4 times. Cont on rem 4 sts until work

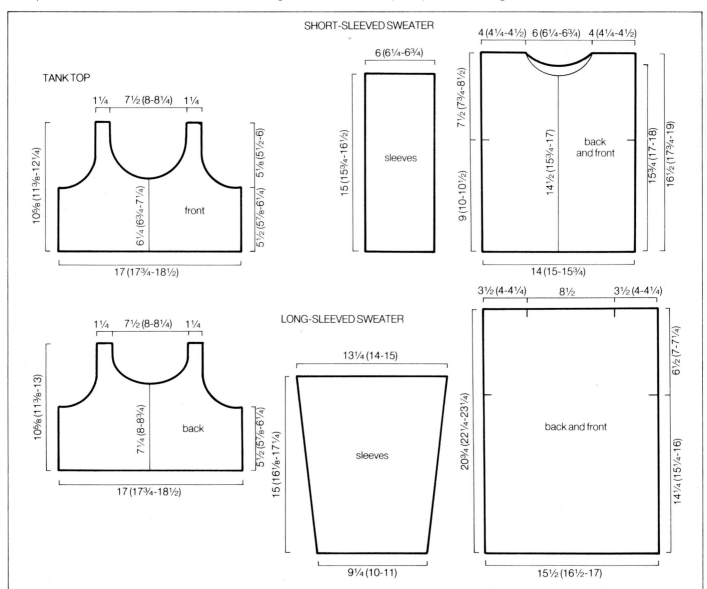

measures 10⅝(11⅜,12¼)in/ (27,29,31cm) from beg. Bind off. Rejoin yarn to neck edge of right back sts and complete as for left back from ** to end reversing shapings.

▦ **Front** Work as for back until 6 rows of armhole shaping have been worked. 43 (46-49) sts.

▦ **Neck Shaping** *1st row* Bind off 2, k until there are 16 (17-18) sts on right needle, leave these for left front, bind off next 7 (8-9) sts, k to end. Bind off 2 sts at beg of foll row. *** Cont to dec 1 st at armhole edge on every other row twice more and *at same time* bind off at neck edge 2 sts on next row and then every other row twice more, then 1 st 4 times. When piece matches back to shoulder edge, bind off. Rejoin yarn to neck edge of left front sts and complete as for right front reversing shapings.

▦ **Finishing** Join shoulder and side seams.

SHORTS

▦ **Back** Beg at waist edge cast on 42 (46-50) sts using smaller needles and work in k 1, p 1 rib for 2⅜in (6cm). Change to larger needles and work in double rib as foll:

▦ *1st row* (right side) K 2, * p 2, k 2; rep from * to end.

▦ *2nd row* P 2, * k 2, p 2; rep from * to end. Rep these 2 rows until work measures 9(9¾,10⅝)in/ (23,25,27cm) from beg.

▦ *Next row* Rib 20 (22-24), bind off 2, rib to end. Cont on 20 (22-24)

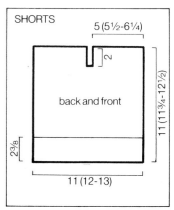

SHORTS

5 (5½-6¼)

2

back and front

11 (11¾-12½)

2⅜

11 (12-13)

ts now rem on needle keeping rib
correct for 2in (5cm) then bind off
n rib. Complete other leg section
n same way.

▨ **Front** Work as for back.

▨ **Finishing** Join side seams.
oin inner leg and crotch seams.

.EG-WARMERS

▨ Beg at lower edge cast on 50
ts using smaller needles and
vork in double rib as given for
horts.

▨ If you are using one color, cont
ntil work measures 15¾in
40cm) from beg then bind off in
b.

▨ If you are using 2 or more
colors, decide on main color and
oind on with this. Work in double

rib * working 3½in (8cm) in main
color then 1½in (4cm) in another
color; * rep from * to * twice more;
then work 1½in (4cm) in main
color.

▨ Bind off in rib. Join back seam.
Make second leg-warmer to
match.

BANDEAU

▨ This is so simple – with only 5
sts to count – that it would make
an ideal learning project for a
complete beginner to knitting.
With smaller needles cast on 5 sts
and work in g st for 27½in (70cm).
Bind off.

LIGHTNING FLASH

Just the thing for a mutual admiration society of two (or more) members: small children love to be dressed like their parents, so this smart sweater in a two-tone pattern with an embroidered multicolored zigzag comes in sizes for adults as well as children. Although a father and son are featured here, the adult version provides a comfortable loose fit for a woman, so you could make a sweater for each member of the family, perhaps changing the background colors to add interest and variety.

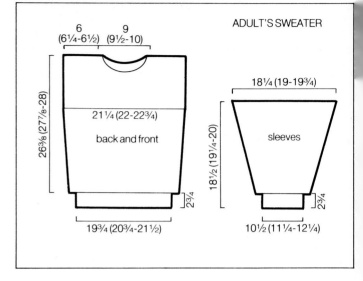

ADULT'S SWEATER

back and front

sleeves

ADULT'S VERSION

CHECKLIST

Materials
Laine Marigold 4 fils: 7(7-8) balls of No 8767, dark gray (**A**), and 6(6-7) balls of No 8673, light gray (**B**). For the lightning flash, small amounts of 4-ply yarn in several different bright colors. Pair each of needles size 2 and 3.

Sizes
Three sizes, to fit chest sizes 38(40-42)in, 97(102-107)cm, normal fit for a man, or 34(36-38)in, 87(92-97)cm, loose fit for a woman. Actual measurements shown on diagram.

Stitches used
Single rib; st st; patt, worked from chart; the lightning flash is embroidered on afterwards by the Swiss darning method explained on page 6 and the placing of the motif is explained below.

Gauge
Over patt using larger needles, 28 sts and 30 rows to 4in (10cm). Work a sample on 33 sts as given for 1st size on back.

INSTRUCTIONS

▦ **Back** With smaller needles and **A**, cast on 131 (137-143) sts and work in rib.
▦ ** 1st row (right side) P 1, * k 1, p 1; rep from * to end.
▦ 2nd row K 1, * p 1, k 1; rep from * to end. Rep these 2 rows until work measures 2¾in (7cm) from beg, ending with a 1st rib row. **
▦ Inc row Rib 7 (10-13), [inc in next st, rib 12] 9 times, inc in next st, rib 6 (9-12), 141 (147-153) sts. Change to larger needles, join **B** and working in st st work patt from chart.
▦ 1st row For 1st and 3rd sizes: k 1 **A**, 1 **B**, 2 **A**, 1 **B**, * 2 **A**, [1 **B**, 1 **A**] 3 times, 1 **B**, 2 **A**, 1 **B**; * rep from * to * ending 2 **A**, 1 **B**, 1 **A**. For 2nd size: k 1 **A**, 1 **B**, then rep from * to * as for 1st size ending 1 **A**.

▦ 2nd row For 1st and 3rd sizes: p 2 **A**, 1 **B**, 1 **A**, * 2 **A**, [1 **B**, 1 **A**] 5 times; * rep from * to * ending 2 **A**, 1 **B**, 2 **A**. For 2nd size: p 1 **A**, rep from * to * in 1st size row ending 2 **A**. Cont in patt as now set for 16 (18-20) more rows then inc 1 st at both ends of next row then every foll 20th row 4 times more working extra sts into patt. Cont on 151 (157-163) sts until piece measures 25⅝in(26⅜in,27⅞in)/(65,67,69cm) from beg, ending with a p row.
▦ **Neck Shaping** 1st row Patt 55 (57-59) and leave these sts of right back on a spare needle, bind off next 41 (43-45) sts, patt to end. Cont on 55 (57-59) sts now rem on needle for left back and work 1 row. Bind off 5 sts at beg of next row and next alt row then dec 1 st at same edge on next 2 rows. Bind off rem 43 (45-47) sts for shoulder

edge. Rejoin yarns to neck edge of right back sts, bind off 5, patt to end. Bind off 5 sts at neck edge on next alt row, dec 1 st at same edge on next 2 rows, work 1 row then bind off rem 43 (45-47) sts.

▦ **Front** Work as for back until piece measures 24(24¾in,25⅝in)/ (61,63,65cm) from beg, ending with a p row.
▦ **Neck Shaping** 1st row Patt 59 (61-63) and leave these sts of left front on a spare needle, bind off next 33 (35-37) sts, patt to end. Cont on 59 (61-63) sts now rem on needle for right front and work 1 row. *** Bind off 4 sts at beg of next row then every other row once, then 2 sts every other row, 3 times; then 1 st twice. Cont on rem 43 (45-47) sts until work matches back to shoulder edge. Bind off. Rejoin yarns to neck edge of left front sts and complete as for right from *** to end.

▦ **Sleeves** With smaller needles and **A** bind on 65 (69-73) sts and work as for back welt from ** to **.
▦ Inc row Rib 5 (1-4), [inc in next st, rib 5 (5-4)] 9 (11-13) times, inc in next st, rib 5 (1-3). 75 (81-87) sts. Change to larger needles and patt.
▦ For 1st and 3rd sizes: work as for 2nd size on back; for 2nd size work as for 1st and 3rd sizes on back. Cont thus in patt until 4 rows have been worked then inc 1 st at both ends of next row then every

foll 6th row 2 (5-8) times then every foll 4th row 24 (21-18) times working extra sts into patt. Cont on 129 (135-141) sts until work measures 18½(19¼,20)in/ (47,49,51cm) from beg. Bind off all sts.

▦ **Lightning** Use oddments of 4-ply yarn in as many bright colors as possible arranging them to suit your taste. Miss the first 22 (24-26) sts at left-hand edge on 1st row of patt on back and using one of the colors embroider over the next 2 sts; on next 2 sts use another color and on foll 2 sts a 3rd color. Move the whole group of 6 sts 1 st over to the right on every row, joining on new colors to give a random effect. Cont moving the group of 6 sts over to the right until a point 12¼(12⅝,13)in/(31,32,33cm) from cast-on edge of back then change direction and move the group back towards the left on every row until the point 19¼(20,20¾)in/(49,51,53cm) above cast-on edge is reached. Now change direction again and cont to top edge. Work similar line on front; this line will end at the neck. On sleeve work a short line beg 16 (18-20) sts from left-hand edge of sleeve and moving to the right 1 st at a time for the first 28 rows then back again for 27 rows to end in same position.

▦ **Neck border** Join right shoulder seam. With right side of

work facing and using smaller needles and **A**, pick up and k 83 (85-87) sts around front neck edge and 68 (70-72) sts across back neck. 151 (155-159) sts. Beg with 2nd row work in rib for 2in (5cm). Bind off loosely in rib.

▦ **Finishing** Join left shoulder

seam and ends of neck border. Fold border in half to wrong side; slip-st bound-off edge to back of picked-up sts. Mark sides 9(9½, 9¾)in/(23,24,25cm) down from shoulder seam for armholes and sew bound-off edge of sleeves between markers. Join side and sleeve seams.

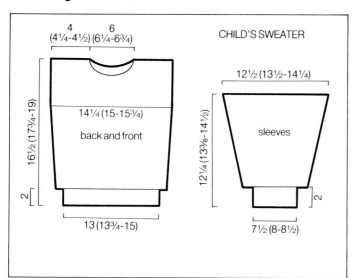

CHILD'S VERSION

CHECKLIST

Materials

*Laine Marigold 4 fils: 3 (3-3) balls of No 8673, light gray (**A**), and 3 (3-3) balls of No 8767, dark gray (**B**). Small amounts of 4-ply yarn for the lightning flash. Pair each of needles size 2 and 5.*

Sizes

Three sizes, to fit ages 4 (6-8) years. Actual measurements shown on diagram.

Stitches used and gauge are the same as for the adult version.

INSTRUCTIONS

▦ **Back** With smaller needles and **B** bind on 87 (93-99) sts and work in rib as on adult's sweater for 2in (5cm), ending with a 1st rib row.
▦ *Inc row* Rib 8 (11-14), [inc in next st, rib 13] 5 times, inc in next st, rib 8 (11-14). 93 (99-105) sts. Change to larger needles and working in st st work patt from chart. All sizes fit in same way as for adult's sweater but note the change of color; light gray is used

for the background and dark gray for the patt. Cont in patt until 14 (16-18) rows have been worked then inc 1 st at both ends of next row then every foll 14th row 3 times more, working extra sts into patt. Cont on 101 (107-113) sts until work measures 15¾(17,18)in/(40,43,46cm) from beg, ending with a p row.
▦ **Neck Shaping** *1st row* Patt 39 (41-43) and leave these sts of right back on a spare needle, bind off next 23 (25-27) sts, patt to end. Cont on 39 (41-43) sts now rem on needle for left back and work 1 row. Bind off 4 sts at beg of next row and next alt row then dec 1 st at same edge on next 2 rows. Bind off rem 29 (31-33) sts for shoulder edge. Rejoin yarn to neck edge of right back sts, bind off 4, patt to end. Bind off 4 sts at same edge on next alt row, dec 1 st at same edge on next 2 rows, work 1 row then bind off rem 29 (31-33) sts.

▦ **Front** Work as for back until piece measures 14½(15¾,17)in/ (37,40,43cm) from beg, ending with a p row.
▦ **Neck Shaping** *1st row* Patt 40 (42-44) and leave these sts of left front on a spare needle, bind off next 21 (23-25) sts, patt to end. Cont on 40 (42-44) sts now rem on needle for right front and work 1 row. ⁕⁕⁕ Bind off 4 sts at beg of next row, 2 sts at same edge every other row 3 times and 1 st every other row, once. Cont on rem sts until work matches back to shoulder edge. Bind off all sts. Rejoin yarns to neck edge of left front sts and complete as for right front from ⁕⁕⁕ to end.

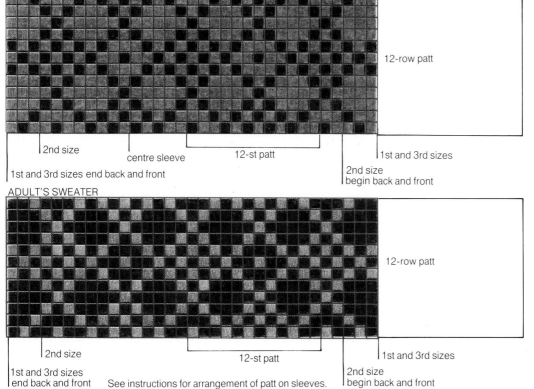

Sleeves With smaller needles and **B** cast on 47 (49-53) sts and work in rib as for adult's sweater for 2in (5cm), ending with a 1st rib row.

Inc row Rib 6 (3-5), [inc in next st, rib 6 (5-5)] 5 (7-7) times, inc in next st, rib 5 (3-5). 53 (57-61) sts. Change to larger needles and work in patt.

1st row 1st size K [1 **A**, 1 **B**] 3 times, * 2 **A**, 1 **B**, 2 **A**, [1 **B**, 1 **A**] 3 times, 1 **B**; * rep from * to * twice more, 2 **A**, 1 **B**, 2 **A**, [1 **B**, 1 **A**] 3 times.

2nd size K [1 **A**, 1 **B**] 4 times, rep from * to * in 1st size row 4 times, 1 **A**.

3rd size K 1 **B**, 2 **A**, [1 **B**, 1 **A**] 3 times, 1 **B** rep from * to * in 1st size row 4 times, 2 **A**, 1 **B**.

All sizes Cont in patt as now set for 4 more rows then inc 1 st at both ends of next row, then every foll 6th row 0 (2-4) times, then every foll 4th row 17 (16-15) times working extra sts into patt. Cont on 89 (95-101) sts until work measures 12¼ (13⅜, 14½)in/ 31,34,37cm) from beg. Bind off all sts.

Lightning Flash Work as for adult's sweater beg the line 22 (24-26) sts from left side edge on 1st patt row of back and front and moving it to the right 1 st on every row. Change direction 6¾ (7½, 8¼)in/(17,19,21cm) above cast-on edge, moving to the left for the next 4 (4¼, 4¾)in/ 10,11,12cm), then move to the right for remainder of back or front. On sleeves begin the line 12 (14-16) sts from left side edge and move right for 24 rows then left for the next 23 rows.

Neck border Join right shoulder seam. With right side of work facing and using smaller needles and **B**, pick up and k 59 (61-63) sts around front neck edge and 46 (48-50) sts across back neck. 105 (109-113) sts. Beg with 2nd row work in rib for 1½in (4cm), then bind off loosely in rib.

Finishing As for adult's sweater placing armhole markers 6¼ (6¾, 7⅛)in/(16,17,18cm) down from shoulder seams.

COMFORTING MOHAIR

Their first day at school, and how hard it is to go inside alone! Soon all these new faces will belong to friends, but in the meantime a little reassurance is needed, so give it in the form of one of these enchanting mohair sweaters. The yellow sweater (style 1) has a shirt-neck opening; the red one (style 2) has contrasting patches and an opening on the left front, while the third version has a cosy kangeroo pocket and ribbed yokes. All are given in three sizes, to fit an older brother or sister as well.

CHECKLIST

Materials
Berger du Nord Kid Mohair: *for Style 1, 3 (4-4) balls of No 7987, bright yellow (**A**) and 1 ball of No 7986, amber (**B**); for Style 2, 3 (4-4) balls of No 7285, bright pink (**A**), 1 ball of No 7862, red (**B**) and 1 ball No 7206, raspberry red (**C**); and for Style 3, 3 (4-4) balls of No 7992, royal blue (**A**), 1 ball of No 7991, lavender (**B**) and one ball of No 7858, blue-green (**C**). Pair each of needles size 3 and 7; 3 buttons each for Style 1 and 2.*

Sizes
Three sizes for each style, to fit ages 4 (6-8) years. Actual measurements shown on diagram.

Stitches used
For all styles: single rib and st st, and for Style 3, k 4, p4 rib, as explained below.

Gauge
Over st st using size 7 needles, 19 sts and 25 rows to 4in (10cm). Work a sample on 25 sts.

INSTRUCTIONS

STYLE 1

▦ **Back** With smaller needles and **B**, cast on 62 (66-70) sts and work in k 1, p 1 rib for 2in (5cm). Change to larger needles and **A**. Work in st st and cont until work measures 9(9¾,10⅝)in/(23,25,27cm) from beg, ending with a p row. ✲✲

▦ **Armhole Shaping** Bind off 3 sts at beg of next 2 rows, 2 sts at beg of next 2 rows and 1 st at beg of next 4 rows. Cont on rem 48 (52-56) sts until work measures 13⅜(14½,15¾)in/(34,37,40cm) from beg, ending with a p row.

▦ **Shoulder Shaping** Bind off 5 (6-7) sts at beg of next 2 rows and 6 (7-8) sts at beg of next 2 rows. Bind off rem 26 sts for back neck.

▦ **Front** Work as for back to ✲✲.

▦ **Armhole Shaping and Front Opening** *1st row* Bind off 3, k until there are 25 (27-29) sts on right needle, leave these for left front, bind off next 6 sts, k to end. Cont on 28 (30-32) sts now rem on needle for right front. Bind off 3 sts at beg of next row, 2 sts at same edge every other row once, then 1 st every other row twice. Cont on rem sts until work measures 12¼(13⅜,14½)in/(31,34,37cm) from beg, ending at the opening.

▦ **Neck and Shoulder Shaping** Bind off 5 sts at beg of next row, 2 sts at same edge every other row twice and then 1 st once. *At same time,* when work matches back to shoulder, ending at side edge, bind off 5 (6-7) sts at beg of next row, work 1 row then bind off rem 6 (7-8) sts.

▦ With wrong side facing rejoin yarn to left front sts, p to end. Bind

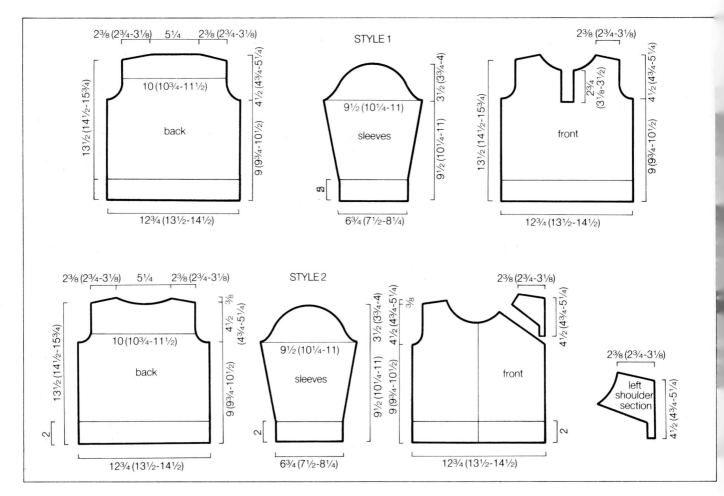

STYLE 1

STYLE 2

off 2 sts of beg of next row and 1 st at same edge every other row twice. Complete as for right front reversing shapings.

Sleeves With smaller needles and **B** cast on 32 (36-40) sts and work in single rib for 2in (5cm). Change to larger needles and **A**. Work in st st but inc 1 st at both ends of every foll 8th row 0 (2-5) times then every foll 6th row 7 (5-2) times. Cont on 46 (50-54) sts until work measures 9½(10¼,11)in/ (24,26,28cm) from beg.

Top Shaping Bind off 2 sts at beg of next 4 rows, 1 st at beg of next 10 (12-14) rows, 2 sts at beg of next 6 rows and 3 sts at beg of next 2 rows. Bind off rem 10 (12-14) sts.

Front borders With smaller needles and **B** cast on 9 sts.
1st row (right side) K 2, * p 1, k 1; rep from * to last st, k 1.

2nd row K 1, * p 1, k 1; rep from * to end. Cont in this rib but make buttonhole.
3rd row K 2, p 1, bind off 3, work to end.
4th row K 1, p 1, k 1, turn, cast on 3, turn, k 1, p 1, k 1. Make 2 more buttonholes each 1(1⅛,1⅜)in/(2.5,3,3.5cm) above bound-off edge of previous one then cont until border measures 2¾(3⅛,3½)in/(7(8,9cm) from beg. Bind off in rib. Work another border omitting buttonholes.

Collar With smaller needles and **B** cast on 75 sts and rep 1st and 2nd rows given for front border until collar measures 5(6-7)cm, 2(2⅜-2¾)in from beg. Bind off in rib.

Finishing Join shoulder seams, sew in sleeves then join side and sleeve seams. Sew front borders to sides of front opening

with buttonhole border to right front for a girl or left front for a boy. Lap buttonhole border over button border and slip-st in place at base of opening. With wrong side of collar to right side of sweater sew bound-off edge to neck edges with a flat join, beg and ending half-way across front borders. Sew on buttons to match.

STYLE 2

Back With smaller needles and **B** cast on 62 (66-70) sts and work in k 1, p 1 rib for 2in (5cm). Change to larger needles and work in st st forming a triangular section in **C** as foll: cut **B** and join on **C** at beg.
1st row K 26 (28-30) **C**, join on **A**, k 36 (38-40) **A**.
2nd row P 37 (39-41) **A**, twist yarns, p 25 (27-29) **C**. Cont working 1 extra st in **A** on every row and 1 st fewer in **C** always twisting yarns when changing

color, until all sts are in **A**. Cont until work measures 9(9¾,10⅝)in/ (23,25,27cm) from beg, ending with a p row.

Armhole Shaping Bind off 3 sts at beg of next 2 rows and 2 sts at beg of next 2 rows then dec 1 st at both ends every other row twice, 48 (52-56) sts. Now begin forming a triangle in **C** at left back.
1st row K 46 (50-54) **A**, join on **C**, k 2 **C**.
2nd row P 3 **C**, twist yarns, p 45 (49-53) **A**. Cont working 1 st extra in **C** on every row, twisting yarns when changing color for remainder of back. At same time, cont until work measures 13⅜(14½,15¾)in/(34,37,40cm) from beg, ending with a p row.

Shoulder and Neck Shaping 1st row Bind off 5 (6-7) sts, k until there are 11 (12-13) sts on right needle, leave these for right back, bind off next 16 sts, k to end. Cont on 16 (18-20) sts now rem at end

of needle for left back. Bind off 5 (6-7) sts at beg of next row and 5 sts at neck edge on foll row. Bind off rem 6 (7-8) sts to complete shoulder slope. Rejoin yarn to neck edge of right back sts, bind off 5, p to end. Bind off rem sts.

▦ **Front** Work as for back until ribbing is completed then change to larger needles and work in st st forming triangle at right front.

▦ *1st row* K 36 (38-40) **A**, join on **C**, k 26 (28-30) **C**.

▦ *2nd row* P 25 (27-29) **C**, twist yarns, p 37 (39-41) **A**. Cont

working 1 st fewer in **C** and 1 st more in **A** on every row until all sts are in **A** then cont until work matches back to armhole ending with a p row.

▦ **Armhole Shaping** *1st row* Bind off 3 sts – left front edge, k to end.

▦ *2nd row* Bind off 3 – right front edge, p to end.

▦ *3rd row* As 1st.

▦ *4th row* Bind off 2, p to end.

▦ *5th row* Bind off 2, k to end.

▦ *6th row* Bind off 1, p to end.
Rep last 2 rows once. This completes armhole shaping at

right front edge. Cont to shape left front edge by binding off 2 sts at beg of next row and every other row 1 (2,3) times. Work 1 row on rem 41 (43-45) sts.

▦ **Neck Shaping** *1st row* Bind off 2, k untll there are 8 sts on right needle, leave these sts on a holder, bind off next 14 sts, k to end. Cont on 17 (19-21) sts now rem on needle for right front and bind off 2 sts at neck edge on next alt row, dec 1 st at same edge on next 2 rows then dec at same edge on every other row twice. Cont on rem 11 (13-15) sts until

work matches back to beg of shoulder, ending at side edge. Bind off 5 (6-7) sts at beg of next row, work 1 row then bind off rem 6 (7-8) sts.

▦ Rejoin **A** with wrong side facing to rem 8 sts of left front, bind off 2, p to end.

▦ *3rd row* Bind off 2, k to last 2 sts, k 2 tog. Dec 1 st at beg of foll row. Bind off rem 2 sts.

▦ **Left Shoulder Section** With larger needles and **C** cast on 5 sts and work in st st for 7 rows then cast on 2 sts at beg of next row and next 3 (4-5) alt rows. Work 2 rows straight then dec 1 st at shaped edge on next row and next alt row. Cont on rem 11(13-15) sts until work measures 4¼(4¾,5⅛)in/(11,12,13cm) along the straight side edge, ending at this edge. Shape shoulder as for right front.

▦ **Sleeves** Using correct colors work as for sleeves of Style 2.

▦ **Finishing and Borders** Join right shoulder seam. Sew shoulder edge of left shoulder section to left back shoulder. With right side of work facing and using smaller needles and **B**, pick up and k 68 (74-80) sts all round neck edge beg on main part of front, then across back neck then along neck edge of left shoulder section. Work in k 1, p 1 rib for 4 rows then bind off in rib.

▦ With right side facing and using smaller needles and **B**, pick up and k 16(18-20) sts along lower shaped edge of left shoulder section, between the points marked **A** and **B** on diagram and 4 sts along edge of neck border. Work as for neck border. Along sloping edge of left front and edge of neck border pick up and k 28 (30-32) sts, using smaller needles and **B**. Work 1 row in rib then make buttonholes.

▦ *Next row* Rib 4, bind off 2, [rib until there are 7 (8-9) sts on right needle after previous buttonhole, bind off 2] twice, rib to end. On foll row cast on 2 sts over each buttonhole. Rib 1 more row then

bind off in rib.

▦ Lap this last border over previous border worked and tack in place. Slip-st the short strip at beg of left shoulder section to wrong side of left front. Sew in sleeves then join side and sleeve seams. Sew buttons to ribbed border of left shoulder section to correspond with buttonholes.

STYLE 3

▦ **Back** With smaller needles and **B** cast on 62 (66-70) sts and work in single rib for 2in (5cm). Change to larger needles and **A**; work in st st and cont until work measures 8⅝(9½,10¼)in/(22,24,26cm) from beg, ending with a p row. Now begin working bands of rib using **C**; wind ball of **C** into 2 balls.

▦ *1st row* K 5 (6-7) **A**, join on a ball of **C**, k 4 **C** to begin band of k 4, p 4 rib, join on another ball of **A**, k 44 (46-48) **A**, join on another ball of **C**, k 4 **C** to begin rib, join on another ball of **A**, k 5 (6-7) **A**. Cont working colors as now set always twisting yarns when changing color. Work 1 row. ∗∗ *At same time* begin armhole shaping. Bind off 3 sts at beg of next 2 rows and 2 sts at beg of next 2 rows.

▦ *7th row* K 0 (1-2) **A**, then using **C**, k 4, p 4, then k 36 (38-40) **A**, then using **C** p 4, k 4, then k 0 (1-2) **A**. Cont with colors as set, dec 1 st at both ends of next row and every other row once, 48 (52-56) sts.

▦ *11th row* K 2 (3-4) **C**, p 4 **C**, k 36 (38-40) **A**, p 4 **C**, k 2 (3-4) **C**. Work 1 row with colors as set.

▦ *13th row* K 2 (3-4) **C**, p 4 **C**, k 4

C, then k 28 (30-32) **A**, k 4 **C**, p 4 **C**, k 2 (3-4) **C**. Cont working 4 extra sts in k 4, p 4 rib using **C**, on every foll 6th row twice more so that there are 18 (19-20) sts in this rib at each side. Cont as now set until work measures 13⅜(14½, 15¾)in/(34,37,40cm) from beg, ending with a wrong-side row.

▦ **Shoulder and Neck Shaping** *1st row* Bind off 6 (7-8), patt until there are 12 (13-14) sts on right needle, leave these for right back, bind off next 12 sts, patt to end. Cont on 18 (20-22) sts now rem at end of needle for left back. Bind off 6 (7-8) sts at beg of next row and 5 sts at neck edge on foll row. Bind off rem 7 (8-9) sts to complete shoulder slope. Rejoin yarn to neck edge of right back sts, bind off 5, patt to end. Bind off rem sts.

▦ **Front** Work as for back to ∗∗.
▦ **Armhole Shaping and Front Opening** *3rd row of patt* With colors as set, bind off 3 sts, patt until there are 22 (24-26) sts on right needle, leave these for right front, bind off next 12 sts, patt to end. Cont on 25 (27-29) sts now rem on needle for right front and bind off 3 sts at beg of foll row. ∗∗∗ Cont forming bands of rib in **C** as at each side of back and *at same time* shape both edges; bind off 2 sts at armhole edge every other row once, then 1 st every other row twice, *at the same time* dec 1 st at neck edge on every foll 4th row 4 (3-2) times then every foll 6th row 1 (2-3) times. Cont on rem sts until work matches back to shoulder ending at side.

▦ **Shoulder Shaping** Bind off 6 (7-8) sts at beg of next row, work 1 row then bind off rem 7 (8-9) sts. Rejoin yarn at neck edge to sts of left front and complete as for right front from ∗∗∗ to end, reversing all shapings.

▦ **Sleeves** Using correct colors work as for sleeves of Style 1.

▦ **Pocket** With larger needles and **C** cast on 32 (36-40) sts and work in st st; work 4 (6-8) rows straight then dec 1 st at both ends of next row then every foll 6th row 4 times more. Cont on rem 22 (26-30) sts until work measures 5⅛(5½,5⅞)in/(13,14,15cm) from beg. Bind off. With right side facing and using smaller needles and **C**, pick up and k 30 (32-34) sts along one side edge of pocket. Work in k 1, p 1 rib for 5 rows then bind off in rib. Work similar border along other side edge of pocket.

▦ **Collar** With smaller needles and **B**, cast on 97 (103-109) sts.
▦ *1st row* (right side) K 2, ∗ p 1, k 1; rep from ∗ to last st, k 1.
▦ *2nd row* K 1, ∗ p 1, k 1; rep from ∗ to end. Rep these 2 rows until work measures 2⅜in (6cm) from beg. Bind off in rib.

▦ **Finishing** Join shoulder seams. Sew bound-on edge of collar around neck edges. Lap left edge of collar over right and slip-st in place to base of opening. Sew in sleeves then join side and sleeve seams. Slip-st pocket to center front ¾in (2cm) above end of ribbing.

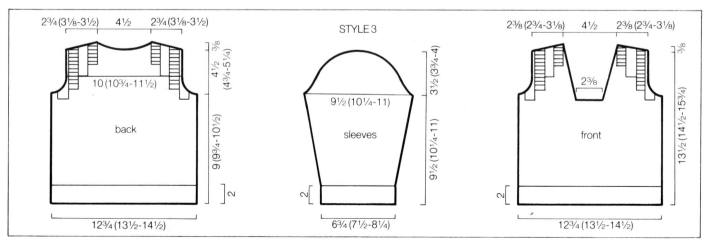

STYLE 3

back — 2¾ (3⅛-3½) 4½ 2¾ (3⅛-3½) — ⅜ — 4½ (4¾-5¼) — 10 (10¾-11½) — 9 (9¾-10½) — 2 — 12¾ (13½-14½)

sleeves — 9½ (10¼-11) — 3½ (3¾-4) — 9½ (10¼-11) — 2 — 6¾ (7½-8¼)

front — 2⅜ (2¾-3⅛) 4½ 2⅜ (2¾-3⅛) — ⅜ — 2⅜ — 13½ (14½-15¾) — 2 — 12¾ (13½-14½)

SCANDINAVIAN SNOWFLAKES

Here's a tough family, all set to go cross-country skiing – Norwegian style – in their richly patterned sweaters; but note that there is plenty of room for additional warm clothing under these outsize knits. The girl wears the same size and shape sweater as the man, though the patterning is different and his version has a roll collar. The child's sweater is a smaller version of the mother's, with the snowflake motifs reversed out. Even the baby joins in with a matching sleeping bag. There are two cozy, double thickness scarfs; other accessories are purchased.

SLEEPING BAG

CHECKLIST

Materials
Laine Marigold 4 fils: *4 balls of No 8098, pale rose* (**A**)*, and 3 balls of No 8623, red* (**B**)*. Pair each of needles size 5 and 7; 6 red buttons.*

Size
One size, to fit baby from birth to 3 months. Actual measurements shown on diagram.

Stitches used
Single rib; st st; patt, *worked from charts as explained below. Strand yarn not in use loosely across wrong side of work to keep fabric elastic and weave in only when working across 5 or more sts. Take great care to position patt correctly each time, by matching center of work to center of chart. Read k rows from right to left and p rows from left to right.*

Gauge
For Sleeping bag and for Man's and Girl's sweaters: over patt using size 7 needles, 23 sts and 24 rows to 4in (10cm). Work a sample on 34 sts.

INSTRUCTIONS

▦ **Back** With larger needles and **A** cast on 65 sts. Beg with a k row, work in st st. Work 4 rows, casting on 4 sts at beg of first 2 rows, then 3 sts at beg of next 2 rows. 79 sts.
▦ Now begin working from charts. * Work 19 rows of Chart 2, 1 row in **A**, 7 rows of Chart 9, 33 rows of Chart 6, 7 rows of Chart 1, * 2 rows in **A**; rep from * to * once more, 1 row in **A**, then 1 row in **B**, *at the same time* casting on 3 sts at beg of first 4 rows, 2 sts at beg of next 2 rows, then 1 st at beg of next 2 rows, work 8 rows straight, then dec 1 st at each end of next and every foll 8th row until 73 sts rem, 142 rows have been worked from beg. Break off **B**.

▦ **Neck Shaping** *143rd row* K 25 and leave these sts of right back on a spare needle, bind off next 23 sts, then k to end. Cont on 25 sts now rem on needle for left back. Change to smaller needles and work in rib.
▦ *1st row* (wrong side) K 1, * p 1, k 1; rep from * to end.
▦ *2nd row* P 1, * k 1, p 1; rep from * to end. Rep these 2 rows once more, then the 1st row again. Bind off in rib. Rejoin **A** to neck edge of right back sts and rib to end. Cont to match first side.

▦ **Front** Work as given for back until 133 rows in all have been worked, keeping patt correct to match back.
▦ **Neck Shaping** *134th row* Patt

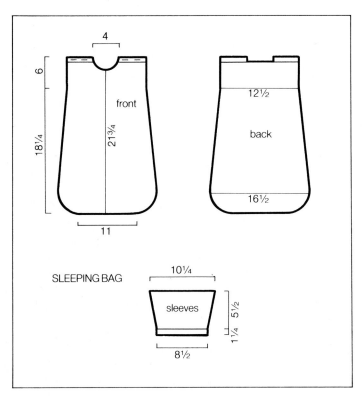

SLEEPING BAG

32 and leave these sts of right front on a spare needle, bind off next 9 sts, then patt to end. Cont on 32 sts now rem on needle for left front; work 1 row straight. Bind off at neck edge 3 sts at beg of next row, 2 sts at beg of foll alt row, then 1 st at beg of foll 2 alt rows. 25 sts. Break off **B**. Work 1 row straight, then work 1 row in rib as on back.

▦ *Next row* Rib 3, [bind off 2 sts, rib 9] twice.

▦ *Next row* Rib to end, casting on 2 sts over each 2 bound off. Work 2 more rows as set, then bind off in rib. Rejoin yarns to neck edge of right front sts, bind off 3 sts and patt to end. Cont to match first side, reversing shaping and position of buttonholes.

▦ **Sleeves** With smaller needles and **A** cast on 51 sts and beg with a 2nd row, work in rib as on shoulders for 1¼in (3cm), ending with a 1st rib row. Change to larger needles. Beg with a k row work in st st. Work 7 rows of Chart 1, 19 rows of Chart 2, 7 rows of Chart 1, then 1 row in **A**, *at the same time* inc 1 st at both ends of the 5th and every foll 6th row until there are 61 sts. Bind off *loosely*.

▦ **Back Neck Border** With smaller needles, **A** and right side facing, pick up and k 41 sts evenly around back neck. Work 5 rows in rib as on shoulders. Bind off in rib.

▦ **Front Neck Border** With smaller needles, **A** and right side facing, pick up and k 49 sts evenly around front neck. Work 1 row in rib as on shoulders.

▦ *Next row* Rib 3, bind off 2 sts, rib 39, bind off 2 sts, rib 3.

▦ *Next row* Rib to end, casting on 2 sts over each 2 bound off. Work 2 more rows as set, then bind off in rib.

▦ **Finishing** At this stage darn in all loose ends. Lay front ribs on top of back ribs and catch down at armhole edge. On each side edge mark a point 5⅛in (13cm) down from shoulder line for armholes and sew bound-off edge of sleeves between marked points. Join side, sleeve and lower edge seams matching patt. Sew on buttons.

GIRL'S SCARF

CHECKLIST

Materials
*Laine Marigold 3 fils: 3 balls of No 8623, red (**A**), and 5 balls of No 8690, banana (**B**). Pair of needles size 5.*

Size
166in (68cm) long and 7¾in (20cm) wide.

Stitches used
As for Sleeping bag.

Gauge
Over patt using needles given, 30 sts and 31 rows to 4in (10cm). Work a sample on 34 sts.

INSTRUCTIONS

▦ **First Section** With smaller needles and **A**, cast on 61 sts. Beg with a k row, work in st st. Work [8 rows of Chart 8, 25 rows of Chart 5, 7 rows of Chart 9, 33 rows of Chart 6, 1 row in **B**, 27 rows of Chart 3, 4 rows in **A**, 1 row in **B**, 2 rows in **A**, 19 rows of Chart 2, 1 row in **B**, 2 rows in **A**] twice. This is now the center of work.

▦ Reverse patt for second half, that is read charts from top to bottom thus making a mirror image of first half. Bind off using **A**.

▦ **Section Section** With smaller needles and **B** cast on 60 sts. Beg with a k row cont in st st until work measures the same as first piece, ending with a p row. Bind off.

▦ **Finishing** At this stage sew in all loose ends. With right side tog, join seams, leaving gap for turning. Turn right side out and close.

1

center

rep 20 sts

2

center

rep 56 sts

3

center

rep 34 sts

4

center

rep 24 sts

5

center

rep 56 sts

6

center

rep 66 sts

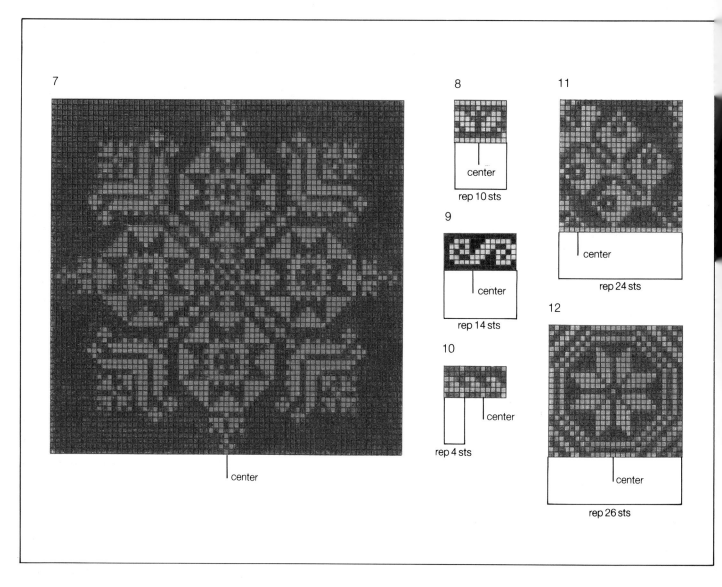

7

8
center
rep 10 sts

9
center
rep 14 sts

10
center
rep 4 sts

11
center
rep 24 sts

12
center
rep 26 sts

center

MAN'S SWEATER

CHECKLIST

Materials
Laine Marigold 4 fils: 9 balls of No 8690, yellow (**A**), *and 6 balls of No 8740, blueberry* (**B**). *Pair each of needles size 2, 5 and 7.*

Size
One size only, to fit 42/44in (107/112cm) chest.

Stitches used and gauge
As for Sleeping bag.

INSTRUCTIONS

▦ **Back** With size 5 needles and **A** cast on 141 sts; work in rib as follows:
▦ *1st row* (right side) P 1, * k 1, p 1; rep from * to end.
▦ 2nd row K 1, * p 1, k 1; rep from * to end. Rep these 2 rows until work measures 2⅜in (6cm) from beg, ending with a 2nd rib row. Change to size 7 needles and beg with a k row work in st st. **※**
▦ Work 19 rows of Chart 2, [1 row in **A**, 7 rows of Chart 9, 33 rows of Chart 6, 7 rows of Chart 1, 1 row in **A**, 19 rows of Chart 2, 2 rows in **A**] twice. 159 rows have been worked in st st. Working in patt from Chart 1:
▦ **※※※ Neck Shaping** *160th row* Patt 60 and leave these sts of left back on a spare needle, bind off next 21 sts, then patt to end. Cont on 60 sts now rem on needle for right back; work 1 row straight. Bind off at neck edge 9 sts at beg of next then every other row once, 42 sts. Work 2 rows straight, then bind off. Rejoin yarns to neck edge of left back sts, bind off 9 sts and patt to end. Cont to match first side, reversing shaping.

▦ **Front** Work as for back until 145 rows have been worked in st st. Keep patt matching back.
▦ **Neck Shaping** *146th row* Patt 65 and leave these sts of right front on a spare needle, bind off next 11 sts, then patt to end. Cont on 65 sts now rem on needle for left front; work 1 row straight.
▦ Bind off at neck edge 5 sts at beg of next row, then 4 sts every other row once; 3 sts every other

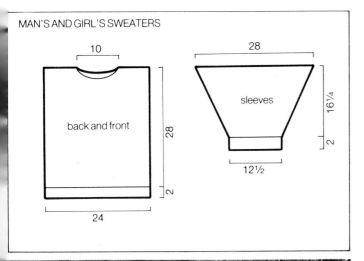

MAN'S AND GIRL'S SWEATERS

back and front

10
28
24
28
2

sleeves

28
12½
16¼
2

row 3 times, 2 sts every other row twice and 1 st once, 42 sts. Work 4 rows straight. Bind off. Rejoin yarns to neck edge of right front sts, bind off 5 sts and patt to end. Cont to work as for first side, reversing shaping.

▦ **Sleeves** With size 5 needles and **A** cast on 73 sts and work in rib as on back ribbing for 2⅜in (6cm), ending with a 2nd rib row. Change to size 7 needles. Beg with a k row work in st st. *** Work 1 row. Now begin working from charts. Work 19 rows of Chart 2, 7 rows of Chart 1, 19 rows of Chart 2, 3 rows in **A**, 7 rows of Chart 9, 33 rows of Chart 6, 7 rows of Chart 1, 3 rows in **A**, *at the same time* inc 1 st at both ends of the 5th and every foll 4th row until there are 81 sts, then every other row until there are 159 sts. Bind off *loosely*.

GIRL'S SWEATER

CHECKLIST

Materials
Laine Marigold 4 fils: *10 balls of No 8685, Van Dyck red* (**A**), *and 5 balls of No 8626, periwinkle blue* (**B**). *Pair each of needles size 5 and 7; set of four double-pointed needles size 5.*

Size
One size, to fit 34/36in (87/92cm) bust very loosely.

Stitches used and gauge
As for Sleeping bag.

INSTRUCTIONS

▦ **Back** Work as given for Man's sweater to **. Work 3 rows in **A**, 1 row in **B**, then 2 rows in **A**. Now begin working from charts. Work 19 rows of Chart 2, 3 rows in **A**, 27 rows of Chart 3, 3 rows in **A**, 26 rows of Chart 4, 25 rows of Chart 12, 26 rows of Chart 11, 2 rows in **A**, 6 rows of Chart 10, 16 rows of Chart 2. 159 rows have been worked in st st.
▦ Working 3 more rows of Chart 2, then 4 rows in **A**, read as given for Man's sweater from *** on back neck shaping to *** on sleeves. Work 2 rows in **A**.
▦ Now begin working from charts. Work 6 rows of Chart 10, 1 row in **B**, 3 rows in **A**, 26 rows of

▦ **Collar** With size 2 needles and **A** cast on 143 sts. Beg with a k row work 4 rows in st st.
▦ *5th row* P to end. Change to size 7 needles and beg with a p row work in st st. Work 4 rows. Now begin working from charts. Beg with row 3, work 17 rows of Chart 2, 3 rows in **A**, 7 rows of Chart 1, 2 rows **A**. Bind off, knitting 2 sts tog across the row.

▦ **Finishing** At this stage sew in all loose ends. Join shoulder seams. On each side edge mark a point 13½in (34.5cm) down from shoulder seam for armholes and sew bound-off edge of sleeves between marked points. Join side and sleeve seams. Join ends of collar to form a circle. Fold cast on edge in on p ridge and slip-st hem. With seam to center back neck, sew bound-off edge to neck.

Chart 4, 25 rows of Chart 12, 26 rows of Chart 11, 2 rows in **A**, 6 rows of Chart 10, 1 row in **A**, *at the same time* inc 1 st at both ends of the 5th and every foll 4th row until there are 81 sts, then every foll alt row until there are 159 sts. Bind off *loosely*.

▦ **Neckband** Join shoulder seams. With set of four double-pointed needles and **A**, pick up and k 160 sts evenly round neck edge. Work 1¼in (3cm) in rounds of k 1, p 1 rib. Bind off *loosely* in rib.

▦ **Finishing** Darn in loose ends. Mark sides 13½in (34.5cm) down from shoulder. Sew bound-off sleeve edges between markers. Join side and sleeve seams.

WOMAN AND CHILD'S SCARF

CHECKLIST

Materials
Woman's version *Malourène Elk: 1 skein each of No 24, turquoise (**A**), and No 601, red (**B**). Pair of needles size 5.*

Child's version *Chat Botté Nénuphar: 3 balls of No 4689, bright green (**A**), 5 balls of No 4600, ruby (**B**). Pair of needles size 5.*

Size
One size only; 71½in (181.5cm) long and 10¾in (27cm) wide. Work a sample on 34 sts.

Stitches used
As for Sleeping bag.

Gauge
For Woman and Child's scarf and sweaters: over patt using needles given, 25 sts and 32 rows to 4in (10cm). Work a sample on 34 sts.

INSTRUCTIONS

▦ With needles given and **A**, cast on 69 sts. Beg with a k row work in st st. Work 5 rows. Now begin working from charts. Work [67 rows of Chart 7, 5 rows in **A**] 8 times. Bind off using **A**.

WOMAN AND CHILD'S SWEATER

CHECKLIST

Materials
*Malourène Elk: 3 (2½) skeins of No 24, turquoise (**A** child, **B** mother), and 1 (5) skeins of No 60, red (**B** child, **A** mother). Pair each of needles size 2 and 5.*

Sizes
Two sizes: small, to fit a child aged 6 to 8 years loosely; large, to fit 36/38in (92/97in) bust. Actual measurements shown on diagram.

Stitches used
As for Sleeping bag.

Gauge
As for Mother and Child's scarf.

▦ With given needles and **B** cast on 68 sts. Beg with a k row cont in st st until work measures the same as first piece, ending with a p row. Bind off.

▦ **Finishing** As for Girl's scarf.

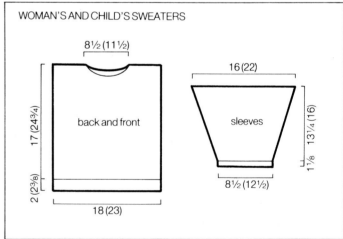

WOMAN'S AND CHILD'S SWEATERS

8½ (11½)

back and front

17 (24¾)

2 (2⅜)

18 (23)

16 (22)

sleeves

13¼ (16)

1⅛

8½ (12½)

INSTRUCTIONS

▦ **Back** With smaller needles and **A** cast on 115 (147) sts and work in rib as on back ribbing of Man's sweater for 2(2⅜)in/(5,6cm), ending with a 2nd rib row.

▦ Change to larger needles and beg with a k row work in st st. Work 2 rows. Now begin working from charts. Work 0 (8) rows of Chart 8, 27 (25) rows of Chart 3 (5), 18 (40) rows in **A**, 67 rows of Chart 7, placing motif in center with sts at each end in **A**, 14 (23) rows in **A**, 0 (27) rows of Chart 3, but reading chart from top to bottom thus reversing patt, 1 row in **A**, 2 rows of Chart 1. 131 (195) rows have been worked in st st. Work 5 more rows of Chart 1, then 2 rows in **A**.

▦ **Neck Shaping** *Next row* Patt 47 (58) and leave these sts of left back on a spare needle, bind off next 21 (31) sts, then patt to end. Cont on 47 (58) sts now rem on needle for right back; work 1 row straight.

Bind off at neck edge 7 sts at beg of next row, then 5 (7) sts at beg of foll 2 alt rows. 30 (37) sts. Rejoin yarn to neck edge of left back sts, bind off 7 sts and patt to end. Cont to work as for first side, reversing shaping.

Front Work as for back until 17 (175) rows have been worked in st st. Keeping patt correct to match back:

Neck Shaping *Next row* Patt 48 (59) and leave these sts of right front on a spare needle, bind off next 19 (29) sts, then patt to end. Cont on 48 (59) sts now rem on needle for left front; work 1 row straight. Bind off at neck edge 2 sts at beg of next and every other row until 30 (37) sts rem. Work 2 (4) rows straight. Bind off. Rejoin yarns to neck edge of right front sts, bind off 2 sts and patt to end. Cont to work as for first side, reversing shaping.

Sleeves With smaller needles and **A** cast on 55 (81) sts and work in rib as on back ribbing for 1¼in (3cm) ending with a 2nd rib row. Change to larger needles. Beg with a k row work in st st. Work 1 row. Now begin working from charts. Work 7 rows of Chart 1, 59 (14) rows in **A**, 0 (67) rows of Chart 7 placing motif in center, 12 rows in **A**, 27 rows of Chart 3 with patt reversed, 2 rows in **A**, *at the same time*, inc 1 st at both ends of the 5th and every foll 6th row until there are 65 (91) sts, then every foll 4th row until there are 103 (141) sts. Bind off *loosely*.

Neckband Join left shoulder seam. With smaller needles, **A** and right side facing, pick up and k 139 (179) sts evenly along neck edge. Beg with a 2nd row, work ¾ (1⅛)in/(2,3cm) in rib as on back rib. Bind off *loosely* in rib.

Finishing At this stage sew in all loose ends. Join right shoulder and neckband seam. On each side edge mark a point 8 (11)in/ (20.5,28cm) down from shoulder seams for armholes and sew bound-off edge of sleeves between marked points. Join sides and sleeve seams.

PAISLEY PAIR

This time it is a father and and daughter who are relaxing together, in sweaters decorated with traditional Paisley motifs, though the design could just as easily be for father and son. Knitted in a luxurious alpaca yarn, both sweaters are identical in their patterning and their drop-shoulder styling, but they are knitted in different color schemes. Back, front and sleeves are each made in two panels which are then joined down the center. Use the colors in separate balls to avoid having to carry long strands across the back.

CHILD'S SWEATER

CHECKLIST

Materials
*Anny Blatt Alpaga: 2 balls of No 2047, larch green (**A**), and 2 balls of No 1497, mulberry (**B**). Anny Blatt No 4: 2 balls of No 1563, emerald (**C**), and 1 ball of No 1564, petrol (**D**). Pair each of needles size 2 and 3.*

Sizes
Two sizes, to fit ages 6 to 7 (8 to 9) years. Actual measurements shown on diagram.

Stitches used
Single rib; st; patt worked from charts as explained below.
*Square No 1 This consists of 4 (6) rows worked in **A**, 41 rows working from Chart No 1, then 3 (5) rows in **A**. When working the patt begin at position indicated according to size, work the sts of patt twice on back and front, once on sleeves, cont to end of row and mark the last st worked; next row will begin at this point.*
*Square No 2 This consists of 4 (6) rows worked in **B**, 4 rows working from Chart No 2, then 3 (5) rows in **B**. When working patt, begin at position indicated according to size, work the sts of patt 3 times on back and front, once on sleeves, cont to end of row and mark the last st worked; next row will begin at this point.*

Gauge
Over st st, using size 3 needles and Alpaga, 29 sts and 37 rows to 4in (10cm). Work a sample on 35 sts; patt will give the same tension.

INSTRUCTIONS

▦ **Back** With smaller needles and **A** cast on 117 (125) sts and work in rib.

▦ *1st row* (right side) P 1, * k 1, p 1; rep from * to end.

▦ *2nd row* K 1 * p 1, k 1; rep from * to end. Rep these two rows until work measures 1½in (4cm) from beg, ending with a 1st rib row.

▦ *Inc row* Rib 10 (6), [inc in next st, rib 15 (13)] 6 (8) times, inc in next st, rib 10 (6). 124 (134) sts. Change to larger needles and patt, dividing work at center.

▦ *1st row* With **A**, k 61 (66), inc in next st, turn and cont on these 63 (68) sts, leaving rem 62 (67) sts on a spare needle. This row counts as 1st row of Square No 1.

▦ Cont on sts for right back and complete Square No 1 then begin a Square No 2; after working 30 (34) rows of this square bind off 3 sts at beg of next row for armhole shaping.

▦ Cont on rem 60 (65) sts until square is completed then work a Square No 1, placing motifs in same positions as on previous square worked in this patt. Cont until 43rd (47th) row of this square has been worked thus ending at center.

▦ **Neck Shaping** Bind off 15 sts at beg of next row and 5 (6) sts at same edge every other row, twice. This completes the square. Bind off rem 35 (38) sts for shoulder.

▦ With right side facing and using **B**, rejoin yarn to group of sts left unworked after rib, inc in 1st st, k to end. Cont on these 63 (68) sts for left back, work rem rows of Square No 2, then work a square No 1 and then a Square No 2. Work armhole shaping 1 row below that of right back and begin neck shaping 1 row below right back; after last shaping row work 1 row then bind off rem 35 (38) sts.

▦ **Front** Work as for back working squares in same positions; right back will thus be left front and vice versa. Work armhole shaping after 30 (34) rows of second square worked, then cont on rem 60 (65) sts until 33 (35) rows of third square have been worked thus ending at center.

▦ **Neck Shaping** Bind off 10 sts at beg of next row, 4 sts at same edge on next 2 alt rows, 2 sts on next 2 (3) alt rows and 1 st on next 3 alt rows. This completes the square. Bind off rem 35 (38) sts for shoulder. Work right front as for left back with squares in same order. Work armhole shaping 1 row below that of left front and begin neck shaping 1 row below left front; after last shaping row work 1 row then bind off rem 35 (38) sts.

▦ **Sleeves** Both alike. With smaller needles and **A** cast on 61 (65) sts and work in rib as on back rib but cont until work measures

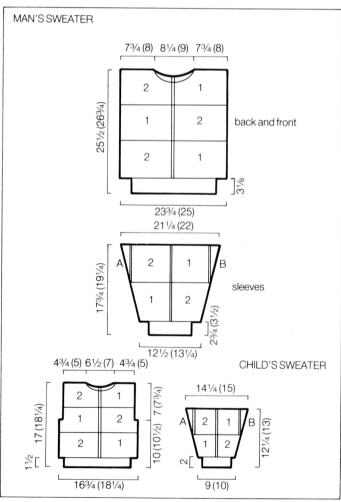

MAN'S SWEATER

7¾ (8) 8¼ (9) 7¾ (8)

2 | 1
1 | 2
2 | 1

25½ (26¾)

back and front

3⅛

23¾ (25)
21¼ (22)

A | 2 | 1 | B
  | 1 | 2 |

sleeves

17¾ (19¼)

2¾ (3½)

12½ (13¼)

4¾ (5) 6½ (7) 4¾ (5)

2 | 1
1 | 2
2 | 1

17 (18¼)

1½

16¾ (18¼)

10 (10½) 7 (7¾)

CHILD'S SWEATER

14¼ (15)

A | 2 | 1 | B
  | 1 | 2 |

12¼ (13)

2

9 (10)

60

2in (5cm) from beg, ending with a 1st rib row.

▦ *Inc row* Rib 6 (2), [inc in next st, rib 11 (9)] 4 (6) times, inc in next row rib 6 (2). 66 (72) sts. Change to larger needles and patt, dividing work at center: change to **B**.

▦ *1st row* K 32 (35), inc in next st, turn and cont on these 34 (37) sts leaving rem sts on a spare needle. Cont working a Square No 2 but inc 1 st at side edge on every foll 6th row 7 times then cont on these 41 (44) sts until this square is completed. Cont without shaping and work a Square No 1; when this is completed bind of all sts. Return to sts left unworked and with right side facing join on **A**, inc in 1st st, k 32 (35). Cont working a Square No 1 with incs at side edge in same way as on first half of sleeve then a Square No 2 without shaping. Bind off.

▦ **Triangular Insertions** With larger needles and **B** cast on 3 sts and work in st st beg with a k row. Work 2 (4) rows then inc 1 st at beg of next row then at same edge on every foll 4th row 11 times more.

MAN'S SWEATER

CHECKLIST

Materials
Anny Blatt Alpaga: *5 balls of No 1770, caramel* (**A**), *and 5 balls of No 1759, pumpkin* (**B**). *Anny Blatt No 4: 5 balls of No 1565, mustard* (**C**), *and 3 balls of No 1566, copper* (**D**). *Pair each of needles size 2 and 3.*

Sizes
Two sizes, to fit 38/40 (42/44)in, 97/102 (107/112)cm, chest. Actual measurements shown on diagram.

Stitches used
Single rib; st st; patt, *worked from charts as explained below.*
Square No 1 *This consists of 4 (6) rows worked in* **A**, *60 rows of patt from Chart No 1, then 6 (8) rows in* **A**. *When working patt begin at position indicated according to size, work the sts of patt 3 times on back and front, once on sleeves, then cont to end of row and mark the last st worked; next row will begin at this point.*
Square No 2 *This consists of 2 (4) rows worked in* **B**, *then 65 rows in patt from Chart No 2, then 3 (5) rows in* **B**. *When working patt begin at position indicated according to size; work the sts of patt 4 times on back and front, twice on sleeves, then cont to end of row and mark last st worked; next row will begin at this point.*

Gauge
As for Child's sweater.

Cont on 15 sts until 48 (52) rows have been worked. Work another triangle in same way but using **A** and reversing shapings. Two triangles are needed for each sleeve.

▦ **Neck Border** With smaller needles and **A** cast on 123 (129) sts and work in k 1, p 1 rib for 10 rows. Bind off loosely in rib.

▦ **Finishing** Join seam at center back, center front and along center of each sleeve making neat backstitch seams. Sew straight side edge of each triangle to sides of the second square worked on each sleeve so that the triangle in **B** is joined to side of Square No 1 and the triangle in **A** is joined to side of Square No 2. Sew bound-off edge of sleeves to sides of armholes and sew armhole shapings to a corresponding depth on sides of sleeves. Join side and sleeve seams. Join ends of neck border; placing seam level with left shoulder seam sew cast-on edge of neck border to neck edges.

INSTRUCTIONS

▦ **Back** With smaller needles and **A** cast on 163 (173) sts and work in rib as for Child's sweater; cont until work measures 3⅛in (8cm) from beg, ending with a 1st rib row.

▦ *Inc row* Rib 6 (8), [inc in next st, rib 14 (12)] 10 (12) times, inc in next st, rib 6 (8). 174 (186) sts. Change to larger needles and patt, dividing work at center.

▦ *1st row* With **A**, k 86 (92), inc in next st, turn and cont on these sts for right back, leaving rem sts on a spare needle. Cont on 88 (94) sts; this row counts as 1st row of Square No 1. Work rem row of this square, then work a Square No 2, the another Square No 1; cont until 65 (69) rows of this square have been worked, ending at center.

▦ **Neck Shaping** Bind off 18 sts at beg of next row and 7 (8) sts at same edge on next 2 alt rows. This completes the square. Bind off rem 56 (60) sts for shoulder edge.

▦ With right side facing and using **B**, rejoin yarn to group of sts left unworked after welt, inc in 1st st, k to end. Cont on these 88 (94) sts for left back; work rem rows of Square No 2, then work a Square No 1, then another Square No 2. Begin neck shaping 1 row before that of right back and after last shaping row work 1 row on rem 56 (60) sts then bind off.

▦ **Front** Work as for back, working squares in same positions; right back will thus be left front and vice versa. Cont until 49 (51) rows of third square are worked thus ending at center.

▦ **Neck Shaping** Bind off 12 sts at beg of next row, 4 sts at same edge on next 2 alt rows, 2 sts on next 4 (5) alt rows and 1 st on next 4 alt rows, completing square. Bind off rem 56 (60) sts for shoulder.

▦ Work right front as for left back with squares in same order; begin neck shaping after 48 (50) rows of third square working as for left front. After last shaping row work 1 row on rem 56 (60) sts. Bind off.

▦ **Sleeves** Both alike. With smaller needles and **A** cast on 71

(77) sts and work in rib as for Child's sweater; cont until work measures 2¾ (3½)in/(7,9cm) from beg, ending with a 1st rib row.

▦ *Inc row* Rib 2 (5), [inc in next st, rib 2] 23 times, rib rem 0 (3) sts. 94 (100) sts. Change to larger needles and patt dividing work at center; change to **B**.

▦ *1st row* K 46 (49), inc in next st, turn and cont on these 48 (51) sts leaving rem sts on a spare needle. Cont working a Square No 2 but inc 1 st at side edge on every foll 6th row 5 (7) times then every foll 4th row 9 (7) times. Cont on 62 (65) sts until this square is completed then work a Square No 1 without shaping. Bind off. Return to sts left unworked, join on **A**, inc in 1st st, k 46 (49). Cont on these 48 (51) sts working a Square No 1 with incs at side edge as on first half of sleeve then work a Square No 2 without shaping. Bind off.

▦ **Triangular Insertions** With larger needles and **B** cast on 3 sts and work in st st beg with a k row. Work 2 (4) rows then inc 1 st at beg of next row then at same edge on every foll 4th row 16 times more. Cont on 20 sts until 70 (74) rows have been worked. Bind off. Work another triangle in same way but using **A** and reversing shapings. Make two triangles per sleeve.

▦ **Neck Border** With smaller needles and **A** cast on 157 (167) sts and work in rib for 10 rows. Bind off loosely in rib.

▦ **Finishing** Join seam along center back, center front and center of each sleeve making neat backstitch seams. Sew straight side edge of each triangle to side edge of the second square worked on each sleeve so that the triangle in **B** is joined to side of Square No 1 and triangle in **A** is joined to Square No 2. On each side edge of main part mark a point 10⅝ (11)in/(27,28cm) down from shoulder seam for armholes and sew bound-off edge of sleeves between markers. Join side and sleeve seams. Join ends of neck border; placing seam level with left shoulder seam sew cast-on edge of border to neck edges.

See instructions for arrangement of patt on squares. On Child's sweater work all 46 rows of chart.

On Man's sweater work all 46 rows then from 1st to 14th row again.

See instructions for arrangement of patt on the squares. On Child's sweater work all 41 rows of chart.

On Man's sweater work from 1st to 24th row twice, then from 1st to 17th rows again.

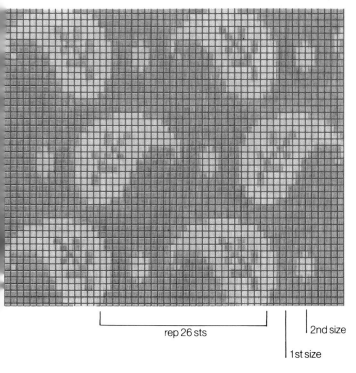

rep 26 sts

2nd size

1st size

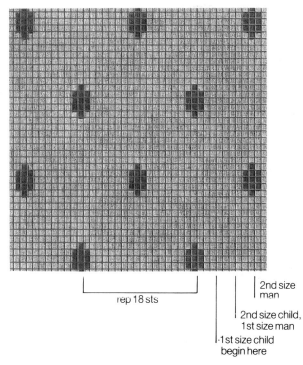

rep 18 sts

2nd size man

2nd size child, 1st size man

1st size child begin here

COUNTRY KIDS

Here is a bold, colorful trio of sweaters designed for lucky boys and girls between the ages of 6 and 14, and ideally suited to children who like the outdoor life and wide open spaces. There are three completely different styles, each with its own distinctive color scheme, but all feature panels of color outlined and separated by narrow stripes, added after the knitting is finished. Colors are suggested, but in practice most children will enjoy choosing their own designs: if they are in need of a holiday project, they could even dye the yarns themselves, in earthy, natural colors.

STYLE 1 (yellow, tan and orange)

CHECKLIST

Materials
*Novita, Florica: 50 (50-100)g each of No 1524, gold (**A**); No 1521, tan (**B**); No 1512, red (**C**); No 1563, pale fawn (**D**); No 1514, pale yellow (**E**), and 50g (all sizes) No 1519, gray (**F**). Pair each of needles size 2 and 5; crochet hook size 3.00mm for working the vertical stripes, or alternatively these can be embroidered in chain stitch, using a tapestry needle.*

Sizes
Three sizes, to fit ages 10 (12-14) years, fitting very loosely. Actual measurements shown on diagram.

Stitches used
Single rib; st st.

Gauge
Over st st using larger needles, 25 sts and 32 rows to 4in (10cm). Work a sample on 30 sts.
The sweater consists of five separate sections, each worked vertically, beg at front and ending at back; ribbing and cuffs are worked on afterwards.

INSTRUCTIONS

▦ **Panel 1** This is for the center front and back. With larger needles and **A**, cast on 43 (47-49) sts and work in st st; cont until work measures 4¾(5⅛,5½)in/ (12,13,14cm) from beg then change to **B** and work 5⅛(5½,5⅞)in/(13,14,15cm) in **B** then change to **C**. Cont until work measures 12¼(13⅜,14½)in/ (31,34,37cm) from beg, ending with a p row.
▦ **Neck Shaping** *1st row* K 12 (13-13) and leave these sts of left front on a spare needle. Bind off next 19 (21-23) sts, k to end. Cont on rem 12 (12, 13) sts for right front. ✶✶ Dec 1 st at neck edge on

next 5 rows then at same edge every other row twice; work 3 rows on rem 5 (6-6) sts. You are now at the shoulder level; cont for right back and work 3 rows straight then inc 1 st at neck edge on next row and next alt row, work 1 row then inc 1 st at same edge on next 5 rows. ✶✶ Work 1 row on these 12 (13-13) sts thus ending at neck edge. Cut yarn and leave sts on a spare needle. Rejoin **C** at neck edge to sts of left front and cont as for right front and back from ✶✶ to ✶✶ reversing shapings. Work 1 row on these 12 (13-13) sts thus ending at side edge.
▦ *Next row* K 12 (13-13), turn, cast on 19 (21-23) sts, turn, then onto same needle, k the 12 (13-13)

64

sts of right back. Cont on these 43 (47-49) sts without further shaping until work measures 7⅞(8⅝,9½)in/(20,22,24cm) from beg of the section in **C**. Work 5⅛(5½,5⅞)in/(13,14,15cm) in **B** then 4¾(5⅛,5½)in/(12,13,14cm) in **A**. Bind off.

▦ **Panel 2** This is for the right front and back, and part of right sleeve. With larger needles and **B** cast on 30 (32-34) sts and work in st st; cont until work measures 3⅛(3½, 4)in/(8,9,10cm) from beg then change to **E**. Cont until work measures 6¾(7½,8¼)in/ (17,19,21cm), from beg, ending with a k row.

▦ **Sleeve Shaping** Cast on 5 sts at beg of next row and next 4 alt rows. Cont on 55 (57-59) sts until you have worked 5½(5⅞,6¼)in/ (14,15,16cm) in **E** then change to **D** and work 10¼(11,11¾)in/ (26,28,30cm), without shaping. Change to **E** and work ¾(1⅛,1½)in/(2,3,4cm), ending at shaped side edge. Bind off 5 sts at beg of next row and next 4 alt rows then cont on rem 30 (32-34) sts until you have worked 5½(5⅞,6¼)in/(14,15,16cm) in **E** then change to **B** and work 3⅛(3½,4)in/(8,9,10cm). Bind off.

▦ **Panel 3** This is for the left front and back, and part of left sleeve. With larger needles and **C** cast on 30 (32-34) sts and work in st st; cont until work measures 3⅛(3½,4)in/(8,9,10cm) from beg then change to **D** and work a further 3½(4,4¼)in/(9,10,11cm) ending with a p row.

▦ **Sleeve Shaping** Change to **E** and cast on 5 sts at beg of next row and next 4 alt rows then cont on these 55 (57-59) sts and work 11¾(12⅝,13⅜)in/(30,32,34cm), ending at shaped edge. Bind off 5 sts at beg of next row and next 4 alt rows. Change to **D** and cont on rem 30 (32-34) sts; work 3¾(4,4¼)in/(9,10,11cm) in **D** then change to **C** and work 3⅛(3½,4)in/(8,9,10cm). Bind off.

▦ **Panel 4** End of right sleeve With larger needles and **C** cast on 5 (6-7) sts and k 1 row; cont in st st and cast on 5 (6-6) sts at beg of

next row then every other row twice more, then 6 (6, 7) sts every other row 3 times; 12 rows have been worked and there are 38 (42-46) sts. Cont without shaping for 8⅞(9⅝,10½)in/(22.5,24.5,26.5cm) ending with a k row. Bind off 6 (6-7) sts at beg of next row then every other row twice, then 5 (6-6) sts every other row 3 times. Bind off rem 5 (6-7) sts.

▦ **Panel 5** End of left sleeve With larger needles and **A** cast on 5 (6-7) sts and p 1 row; work as for Panel 4 reversing shapings by working cast-on and bind-off sts at beg of k rows.

▦ **Neck border** With smaller needles and **C** cast on 96 (100-104) sts and work in single rib for 1⅛in (3cm). Bind off loosely in rib.

▦ **Finishing and stripes** Sew straight side edge of Panel 2 to left-hand edge of Panel 1 and sew corresponding edge of Panel 3 to other side edge of Panel 1, making flat seams. Sew longer side edge of Panel 4 to outer edge of Panel 2, and sew longer side edge of Panel 5 to outer edge of Panel 3. Along seams joining the panels, work 2 lines of chain-st using **F**; either work with the crochet hook or embroider the lines, placing them close tog to hide seams. Ensure that all lines run in same direction from cast-on to bound-off edges.

▦ **Welts and cuffs** With right side of work facing and using smaller needles and **C**, pick up and k 100 (108-116) sts across lower edge of back and work in single rib for 2in (5cm). Bind off loosely in rib. Work front ribbing in same way.

▦ With right side of work facing and using smaller needles and **C**, pick up and k 54 (58-62) sts across outer edge of right sleeve. Work in single rib for 2¾in (7cm) then bind off loosely in rib. Work left cuff in same way.

▦ **Finishing** Join entire side and sleeve seams. Join ends of neck border and sew cast-on edge all round neck edge placing seam at left side of neckline.

STYLE 2 (red, orange and brown)

CHECKLIST

Materials
Novita Florica: *100g each of No 1542, light brown (**A**); No 1513, rust (**B**), and No 1512, orange (**C**); 50(50-100)g each of No 1545, bright red (**D**), and No 1539, geranium (**E**), and 50g each of 1534, dark brown (**F**), and No 1548, dark red (**G**). Pair each of needles size 2 and 5.*

Sizes
Three sizes, to fit ages 6 (8-10) years. Actual measurements shown on diagram.

Stitches used
Single rib; st st. *For the arrangement of colors on back and front see instructions; when changing color during a row always twist yarns on wrong side, picking up the new color from underneath the one previously used.*

Gauge
Over st st using size 5 needles, 25 sts and 32 rows to 4in (10cm); work a sample on 30 sts.

INSTRUCTIONS

▦ **Back** With smaller needles and **A** cast on 90 (96-102) sts and work in single rib for 2in (5cm), working 5 incs evenly spaced along last row, 95 (101-107) sts. Change to larger needles and cut off **A**; work in st st with colors arranged as foll, joining on **C** at beg.

▦ *1st row* K 45 (48-51) **C**, join on a small ball of **F** and k 5 **F**, join on a ball of **B** and k 45 (48-51) **B**.

▦ *2nd row* P 45 (48-51) **B**, twist yarns, p 5 **F**, twist yarns, p 45 (48-51) **C**. Cont as now set until work measures 9(9½,9¾)in/ (23,24,25cm) from beg, ending with a p row. Cut off all colors and join on **F** at beg. Work 6 rows in **F**, cut **F** and join on **D** at beg. Cont as foll:

▦ 1st row K 45 (48-51) **D**, join on small ball of **F** and k 5 **F**, join on a ball of **E** and k 45 (48-51) **E**.

▦ *2nd row* P 45 (48-51) **E**, twist yarns, p 5 **F**, twist yarns, p 45 (48-51) **D**. Cont with colors as now set until work measures 17(18,19¼)in/(43,46,49cm) from beg, ending with a p row.

▦ **Neck Shaping** *1st row* K 36 (38-40) and leave these sts of right back on a spare needle, bind off next 23 (25-27) sts using correct colors, k to end. Cont on 36 (38-

40) sts now rem on needle for left back, using **E**; dec 1 st at neck edge on next row, bind off 4 sts at beg of foll row then p 1 row without shaping. Bind off rem 31 (33-35) sts for shoulder edge. Rejoin **D** to neck edge of right back sts, bind off 4, p to end. Dec 1 st at neck edge on next row then work 1 row straight. Bind off rem 31 (33-35) sts.

▦ **Front** Work as for back until work measures 14½(15¾,17)in/ (37,40,43cm) from beg, ending with a p row.

▦ **Neck Shaping** *1st row* K 41 (43-45) and leave these sts of left front on a spare needle, bind off next 13 (15-17) sts, k to end. Cont on 41 (43-45) sts now rem on needle for right front, using **E**, and work 1 row. ** Bind off 3 sts at beg of next row, 2 sts at same edge every other row twice, then 1 st on every other row 3 times. Cont on rem 31 (33-35) sts until work matches back to shoulder edge. Bind off. Rejoin **D** to neck edge of left front sts and complete as for right front from ** to end.

▦ **Right Sleeve** With smaller needles and **A** cast on 48 (50-52) sts and work in single rib for 1⅛in (3cm) working 4 (5-6) incs evenly spaced along last row. 52 (55-58)

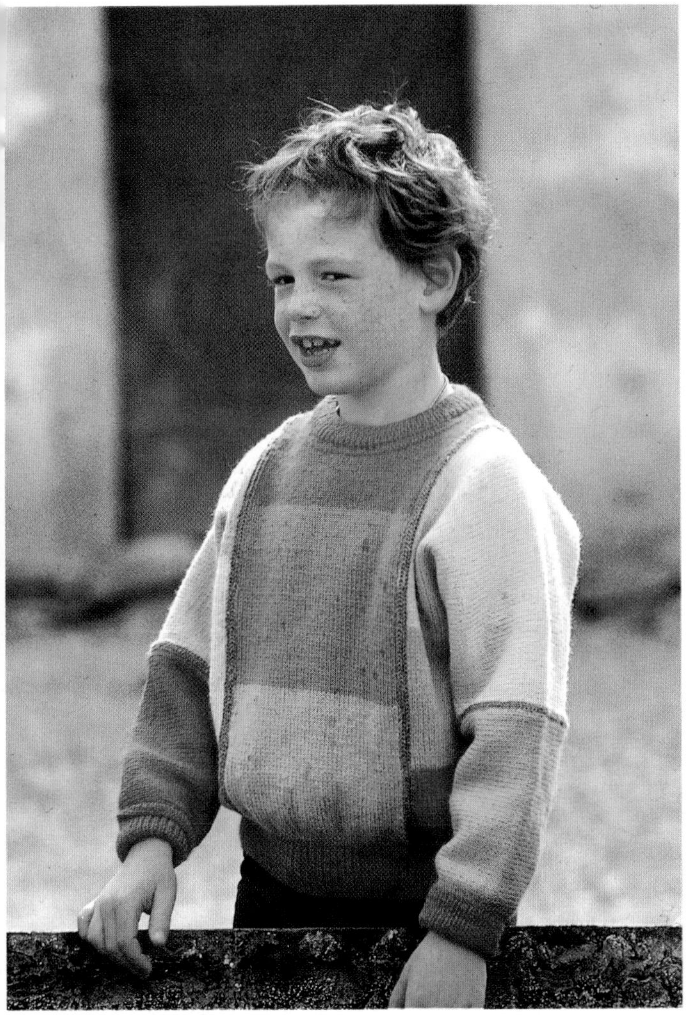

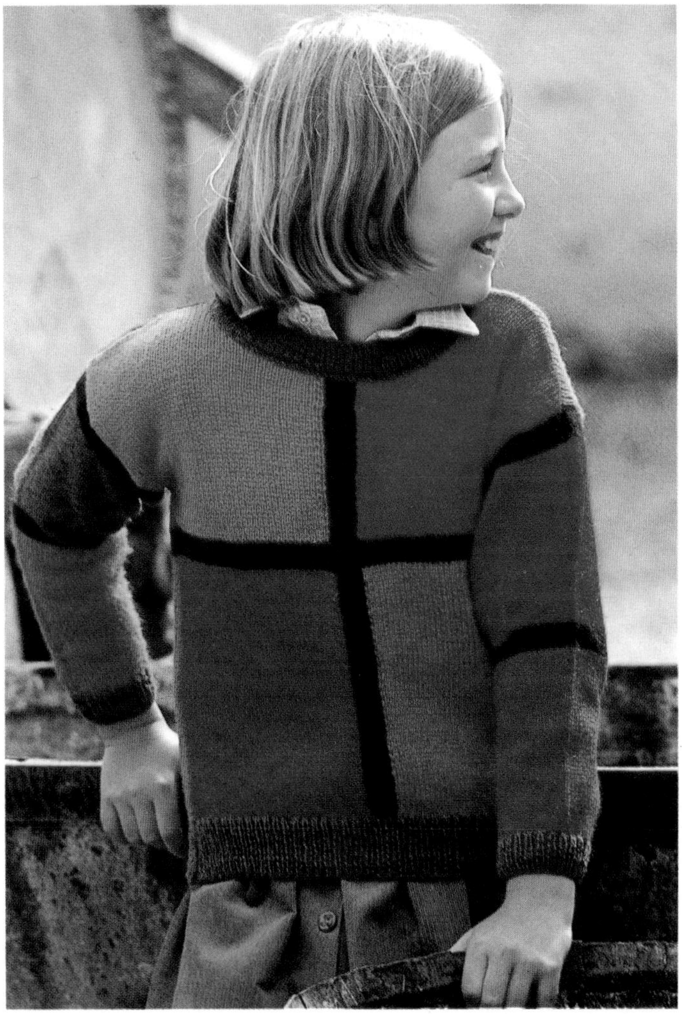

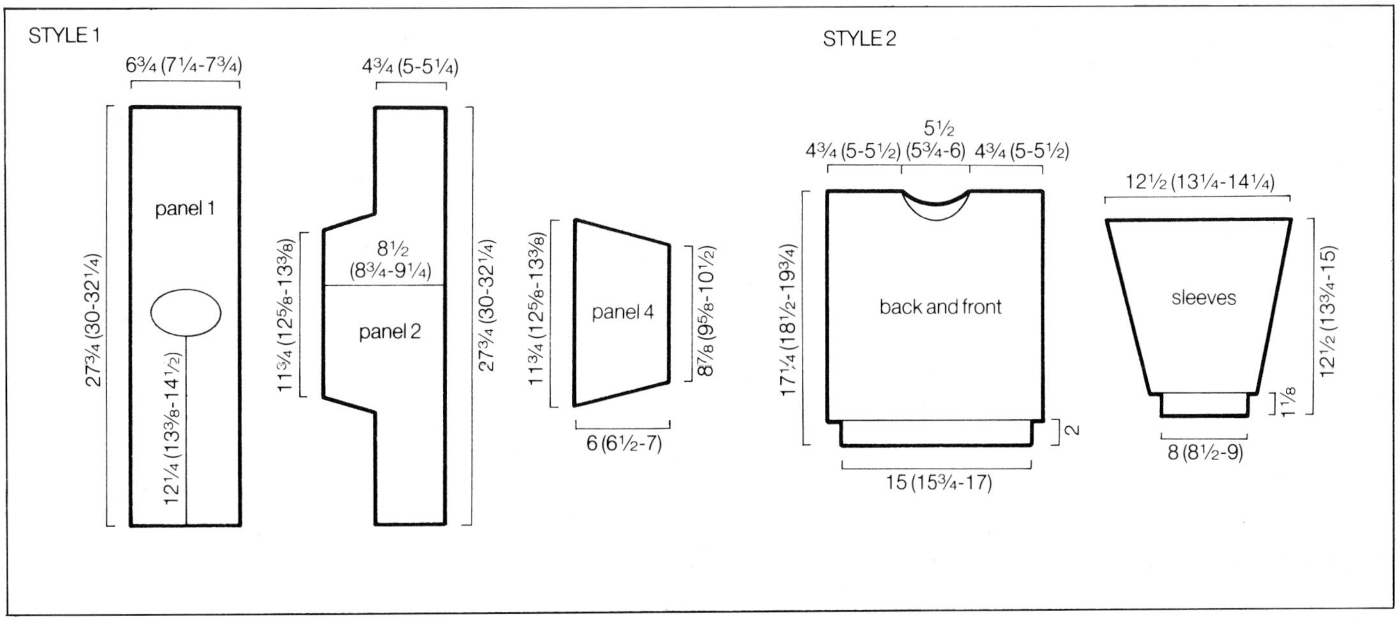
STYLE 1
6¾ (7¼-7¾)
panel 1
27¾ (30-32¼)
12¼ (13⅜-14½)
4¾ (5-5¼)
8½
(8¾-9¼)
panel 2
11¾ (12⅝-13⅜)
27¾ (30-32¼)
panel 4
11¾ (12⅝-13⅜)
8⅞ (9⅝-10½)
6 (6½-7)
STYLE 2
5½
4¾ (5-5½) (5¾-6) 4¾ (5-5½)
back and front
17¼ (18½-19¾)
2
15 (15¾-17)
12½ (13¼-14¼)
sleeves
12½ (13¾-15)
1⅛
8 (8½-9)

sts. Change to larger needles and **C**. Work in st st and inc 1 st at both ends of every foll 6th row 12 (15-16) times then every foll 4th row twice for *1st size only; at same time*, when work measures 6¼(7⅛,7⅞)in/(16,18,20cm) from beg cut off **C** and work 6 rows in **F** then change to **A** and cont until all incs are completed. Cont on these 80 (85-90) sts until work measures 11¾(13,14⅛)in/(30,33,36cm) from beg. Work 6 rows in **F** then bind off all sts.

■ **Left Sleeve** Work as for right sleeve but work the first wide section after cuff in **B** and after the band of **F** work the next section in **G** ending with 6 rows in **F** as on

right sleeve. Bind off.

■ **Neck border** With smaller needles and **A** cast on 96 (100-104) sts and work in single rib for 7 rows. Bind off loosely in rib.

■ **Finishing** Join shoulder seams. Pin bound-off edge of sleeves to sides of sweater placing center of sleeve level with shoulder seam and ensuring that sides of sleeves reach to same position on patt at each side. Sew in place as pinned then join side and sleeve seams matching **F** stripes. Join ends of neck border and sew bound-on edge to neck edges, placing seam level with left shoulder seams.

STYLE 3 (gray, blue, green)

CHECKLIST

Materials
*Novita Fauna: 150g each of No 2019, green (**A**), and No 2024, mid-blue (**B**), and 100g each of No 2006, gray (**C**), and No 2021, royal blue (**D**). Quality Florica: 50g of No 1531, navy (**E**). The latter yarn is used double throughout. Pair each of needles size 5 and 7; a crochet hook size 4.00mm for working the vertical stripes, or alternatively these can be embroidered in chain stitch, using a tapestry needle.*

Sizes
Three sizes, to fit ages 8 (10-12) years. Actual measurements shown on diagram.

Stitches used
Single rib; st st; check patt as explained below. Only the horizontal stripes are worked in; all the vertical stripes are added afterwards.

Gauge
Over st st using size 7 needles, 18 sts and 25 rows to 4in (10cm). Work a sample on 24 sts.
Note: *The color **E** is used double throughout; wind the yarn into 2 equal balls then rewind these tog into a double thickness ball which will be easier to use. When working the check patt, take care always to twist yarns around each other when changing color during a row, picking up the new color from under the color previously used.*

INSTRUCTIONS

■ **Main part** Beg at lower edge of front cast on 76 (78-82) sts using smaller needles and **C**. Work in k 1, p 1 rib for 2in (5cm) working 5 (6-5) incs evenly spaced along last row, 81 (84-87) sts. Change to larger needles and patt.
■ *1st row* K 27 (28-29) **C**, join on **D** and k 27 (28-29) **D**, join on **A**

and k 27 (28-29) **A**.
■ *2nd row* P 27 (28-29) **A**, twist yarns, p 27 (28-29) **D**, twist yarns, p 27 (28-29) **C**. Cont in patt as now set until you have worked 5½(5⅞,6¼)in/(14,15,16cm) in patt, ending with a p row. Cut off all colors and work 2 rows st st in **E**. Cut **E** and join on **B** at beg; cont as folls:
■ *1st row* K 27 (28-29) **B**, join on

A, k 27 (28-29) **A**, join on **C**, k 27 (28-29) **C**. Cont with colors as set until this panel is same length as previous panel, ending with a p row. Cut off all colors and work 2 rows st st in **E**; cut **E** and join on **C** at beg. Start new panels working 1st panel in **C**, 2nd panel in **B** and 3rd panel in **D**. Cont as now set for 2¾(3⅛,3½)in/(7,8,9)cm, ending with a p row.
■ **Neck Shaping** *1st row* Keeping colors correct, k 33 (34-35) and leave these sts of left front on a spare needle, bind off next 15 (16-17) sts, k to end. Cont on 33 (34-35) sts now rem on needle for right front and work 1 row. Bind off 3 sts at beg of next row, 2 sts at same edge every other row once, then 1 st every other row once. Cont on rem sts using **D** only until this panel is same length as previous panel, ending with a p row. Cut **D** and join on **E**; work 2 rows st st in **E** to mark shoulder line then cont for right back. Change to **C** and cont in st st casting on 3 sts at beg of next row and next alt row working these extra sts in **B**. P 1 row on these 33 (34-35) sts thus ending at neck edge. Cut **B** and leave these sts for the present.
■ With wrong side facing rejoin **B** to neck edge of left front sts, bind off 3, p to end using correct colors. Bind off 2 sts at neck edge every other row once, then 1 st every other row once then cont on rem 27 (28-29) sts using **C** only until

this panel is same length as previous panels, ending with a p row. Cut **C** and work 2 rows st st in **E** for shoulder line then cont for left back. Join on **A** and k 1 row then cast on 3 sts at beg of next row and next alt row working these extra sts in **B**.
■ *Next row* K 27 (28-29) **A**, twist yarns, k 6 **B**, turn, cast on 15 (16-17), turn then working sts of right back k 6 **B**, twist yarns, k 27 (28-29) **C**. Cont across all sts until side panels are same length as previous panels ending with a p row then work 2 rows st st in **E**. Start new panels working 1st panel in **B**, 2nd panel in **D** and 3rd panel in **A** and when these are same length as before work 2 rows st st in **E**. For last line of panels work 1st panel in **A**, 2nd panel in **C** and 3rd panel in **B**. Cont until these are same length as before ending with a p row. Cut all colors and join on **C**. K 1 row working 5 (6-5) decs evenly spaced, 76 (78-82) sts. Change to smaller needles and work in k 1, p 1 rib for 2in (5cm). Bind off in rib.

■ **Right Sleeve** With smaller needles and **C** cast on 40 (42-44) sts and work in k 1, p 1 rib for 2in (5cm) working 4 incs evenly spaced along last row, 44 (46-48) sts. Change to larger needles and patt joining on **A** at beg.
■ *1st row* K 22 (23-24) **A**, join on **D**, k 22 (23-24) **D**. Cont with colors as set twisting yarns at center and

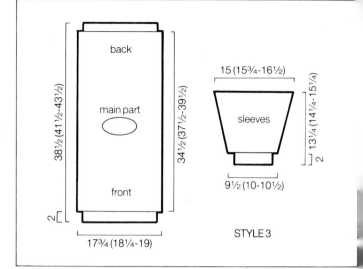

back

main part

front

38½ (41½-43½)

34½ (37½-39½)

2

17¾ (18¼-19)

15 (15¾-16½)

sleeves

13¼ (14¼-15¼)

2

9½ (10-10½)

STYLE 3

work 4 (6-8) more rows then inc 1 st at both ends of next row, then every foll 4th row 4 times more so that there are 27 (28-29) sts in each color. Cont until work measures 5½(5⅞,6¼)in/ (14,15,16cm) from beg of patt ending with a p row then cut colors and work 2 rows in **E**. Now start new panels joining on **C** at beg.

▦ *1st row* K 27 (28-29) **C**, join on **B** and k 27 (28-29) **B**. Cont with colors as set for 3 more rows. Now join on a small ball of **D** at each side and working all extra sts in **D** inc 1 st at both ends of next row then every foll 4th row 6 (7-8) times more. Cont on 68 (72-76) sts until panels are same length as before. Work 2 rows st st in **E**. Bind off.

▦ **Left Sleeve** Work as for right sleeve but with colors as foll: after the cuff work 1st panel in **D** and 2nd panel in **B**. After the stripe in **E** work 1st panel in **C** and 2nd panel in **A** and work all the extra sts at sides in **D**. Complete as for right sleeve.

▦ **Neck border** With smaller needles and **C** cast on 84 (86-88) sts and work in single rib for 1⅛in (3cm). Bind off in rib.

▦ **Vertical stripes** These can either be worked with the crochet hook working in line of slip-sts or else embroidered using a tapestry needle and working a line of chain-st. Beg at bottom of patt on front and using **E** work 2 lines next to each other at the change of color on each panel; cont lines until the center panels are eliminated at the neck and begin again on back. Work similar lines along center of each sleeve and at the change of color where the small sections are worked in **D** at top of sleeves.

▦ **Finishing** Pin bound-off edge of sleeves to sides of sweater with sleeves at correct side edges and matching center vertical stripe on sleeves to the stripe at shoulder line. Sew in place, then join side and sleeve seams matching stripes. Join ends of neck border. Sew cast-on edge to neck edges placing seam at left of neckline level with the shoulder stripe.

TWEEDY FAMILY

This family set is modeled on the British country style – all tweeds and casual elegance – but with that extra plus factor of French chic and color sense. From a sweater for the youngest member of the family, to a cardigan for the head of the clan, all are worked in straightforward block designs, with edges and borders (apart from the girl's sweater) finished in contrast bands of crochet. All are knitted in the same tweedy yarn, but there are different color schemes and patterns, and the sweaters vary in details.

MAN'S CARDIGAN

CHECKLIST

Materials
La Droguerie Tweed: 350(400)g of green (A). Surnaturelle: 150(150)g of pale yellow (B), 60g of apricot and 30g of silver gray. Pair each of needles size 2 and 7; small size crochet hook; 4 buttons.

Sizes
Two sizes, to fit 38/40(42/44)in, 97/102(107/112)cm, chest. Actual measurements shown on diagram.

Stitches used
Single rib; st st; patt, worked from charts as explained below. Strand yarn not in use loosely across wrong side of work to keep fabric elastic and weave in only when working across 5 or more sts. Take great care to position patt correctly each time. Read k rows from right to left and p rows from left to right.

Gauge
Over patt using size 7 needles, 25 sts and 25 rows to 4in (10cm). Work a sample on 30 sts.

INSTRUCTIONS

▦ **Back** With smaller needles and **B**, cast on 137 (149) sts. Break off **B**, join in **A** and work in rib.
▦ *1st row* (right side) P 1, * k 1, p 1; rep from * to end.
▦ *2nd row* K 1, * p 1, k 1; rep from * to end. Rep these 2 rows until work measures 2in (5cm) from beg, ending with a 2nd rib row and inc one st in center of last row. 138 (150) sts. Change to larger needles and beg with a k row work in st st. Cont in patt from Chart until work measures 14½(15⅜)in/ (37,39cm) from beg, ending with a p row.
▦ **Raglan Shaping** Keeping patt correct, dec one st at each end of next 43 (51) rows, then every other row until 38 (40) sts rem, ending

with a p row. Bind off.

▦ **Pocket Linings** (make 2) With larger needles and **A** cast on 33 (35) sts. Beg with a k row cont in st st until work measures 3½(4)in/ (9,10cm) from beg, ending with a p row. Leave sts on a spare needle.

▦ **Left Front** With smaller needles and **B** cast on 69 (75) sts. Break off **B**, join in **A** and work in rib as on back rib for 2in (5cm), ending with a 2nd rib row. Change to larger needles and work in st st. Cont in patt from chart until work measures 5½(6)in/(14,15cm), from beg, ending with a p row.
▦ **Place Pocket** *Next row* Patt 18 (20), slip next 33 (35) sts on to a holder, then with right side facing patt across sts of first pocket

lining, patt to end. Cont until work measures 11(11¾)in/(28,30cm) from beg, ending with a k row.

▦ **Front Shaping** Keeping patt correct, dec one st at beg of next and every foll 4th row until 17 (18) sts in all have been dec at front edge, *at the same time,* when work measures the same as back to armholes, ending with a p row, *for 2nd size only* bind off 3 sts at beg of next and then every other row twice more. *For both sizes* dec one st at armhole edge on every row until 2 sts rem. Bind off.

▦ **Right Front** Work to match left front, reversing all shaping and position of patt.

▦ **Right Sleeve** With smaller needles and **B** cast on 47 (53) sts. Break off **B** join in **A** and work in rib as on back welt for 1¼in (3cm) ending with a 2nd rib row and inc 5 sts evenly across the last row. 52 (58) sts. Change to larger needles and work in st st. Cont in patt from chart; inc one st at each end of the 3rd and every foll 3rd row until there are 120 (130) sts. Cont without shaping until work measures 18½(19¼)in/ (47,49cm), from beg, ending with a p row.

▦ **Top Shaping** *Next row* Bind off 1 (2) sts, patt to last 2 sts, k 2 tog.
▦ *Next row* P 2 tog, patt to last 2 sts, p 2 tog tbl. Rep these 2 rows twice more. Keeping patt correct, dec one st at both ends of next 37 (45) rows. *For first size* only, cont to dec at right hand edge (front) on every row and at left hand edge (back) on every foll alt row until 25 sts rem.
▦ *Next row* Patt to last 2 sts, p 2 tog tbl.
▦ *For both sizes, next row* Bind off 4 sts, patt to last 2 sts, k 2 tog.
▦ *Next row* Patt to end. Rep these 2 rows 3 times more. Bind off rem 4 sts.

▦ **Left Sleeve** Work to match right sleeve, reversing top shaping.

▦ **Button Band** Join raglan seams. With smaller needles and **A** cast on 12 sts and work in rib.
▦ *1st row* (right side) * K 1, p 1; rep from * to end.

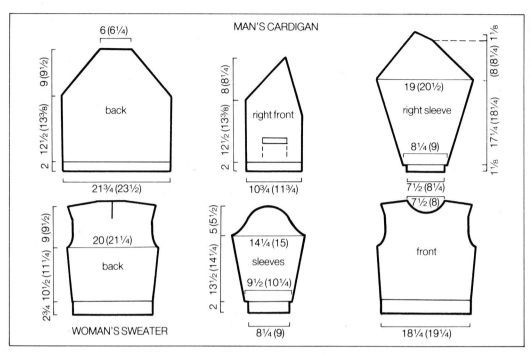

▦ Rep this row until band, when slightly stretched, reaches up right front edge and around to center back neck. Bind off in rib. Tack band in place; with pins mark position of buttons, 1st to come ½in (1cm) from cast on edge, 2nd to come just below beg of front shaping, with 2 more spaced evenly between these.

▦ **Buttonhole Band** Work as given for button band, making buttonholes to correspond with positions of pins as foll: (right side) rib 4, bind off next 4 sts, rib to end.
▦ *Next row* Rib to end, casting on 4 sts over the 4 bound off.

▦ **Pocket Tops** With smaller needles, **A** and right side facing, k to end across sts on holder working twice into first and last sts. 35 (37) sts. Beg with a 2nd row, work ¾in (2cm) in rib as on back ribbing. Bind off *loosely* in rib.

▦ **Finishing** Darn in all loose ends. Join side and sleeve seams. Sew on front bands, joining ends at center back neck. Sew down pocket tops and pocket linings. With right side facing and **B** crochet 1 slip-st row at pocket tops and edge of front bands. Sew on buttons.

WOMAN'S SWEATER

CHECKLIST

Materials
La Droguerie Tweed: *320(350)g of rose* (**A**), *and 40 g each of orange and green. Surnaturelle: 20g of rose* (**B**). *Pair each of needles size 2 and 7; small size crochet hook; 2 pink buttons.*

Sizes
Two sizes, to fit 34/36 (38/40)in, 87/92 (97/102)cm bust. Actual measurements shown on diagram.

Stitches used and gauge
As for Man's cardigan.

INSTRUCTIONS

▦ **Back** With smaller needles and **A**, cast on 115 (123) sts and work in rib as on back ribbing of Man's cardigan until work measures 2¾in (7cm) from beg, ending with a 2nd rib row. Change to larger needles and beg with a k row work in st st. Cont in patt from chart, inc 1 st at both ends of the 9th and every foll 10th row until there are 127 (135) sts. Cont without shaping until piece measures 13⅜(14¼)in/(34,36cm), from beg, ending with a p row.
▦ **Armhole Shaping** Keeping patt correct, bind off 4 sts at beg of next 2 rows, 3 sts at beg of next 2 rows, 2 sts at beg of next 2 rows, then 1 st at beg of next 2 rows. Work 2 rows straight. Dec 1 st at both ends of next and foll 4th row. 103 (111) sts. Cont without shaping until work measures 18½(19¾)in/(47,50cm) from beg, ending with a p row. ※※.
▦ Inc 1 st at both ends of next and foll 4th row. Work 3 rows straight.
▦ **Divide for Opening** *Next row* Inc in first st, patt 52 (56) and leave these sts of right back on a spare needle, bind off 1 st, patt to last st, inc in last st. Cont on 54 (58) sts now rem on needle for left back. Cont as set, inc 1 st at armhole edge on every 4th row until there are 57 (61) sts. Cont without

BABY'S SWEATER

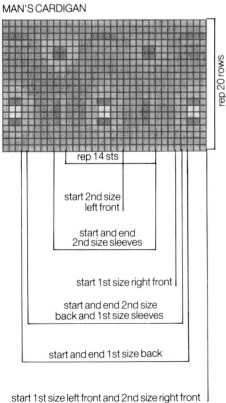

rep 24 rows

rep 12 sts

start and end
1st size back

start and end
3rd size sleeves

start and end 2nd size back

start and end 1st size sleeves

start and end 3rd size back

start and end 2nd size sleeves

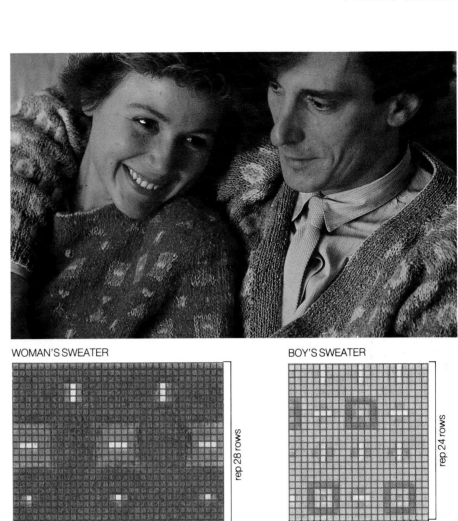

MAN'S CARDIGAN

rep 20 rows

rep 14 sts

start 2nd size
left front

start and end
2nd size sleeves

start 1st size right front

start and end 2nd size
back and 1st size sleeves

start and end 1st size back

start 1st size left front and 2nd size right front

WOMAN'S SWEATER

rep 28 rows

rep 14 sts

start and end 2nd size sleeves

start and end 2nd size back

start and end 1st size back

start and end 1st size sleeves

BOY'S SWEATER

rep 24 rows

rep 12 sts

start and end
2nd size sleeves

start and end
1st and 3rd size back

start and end
3rd size sleeves

start and end 2nd size
back and 1st size sleeves

GIRL'S SWEATER

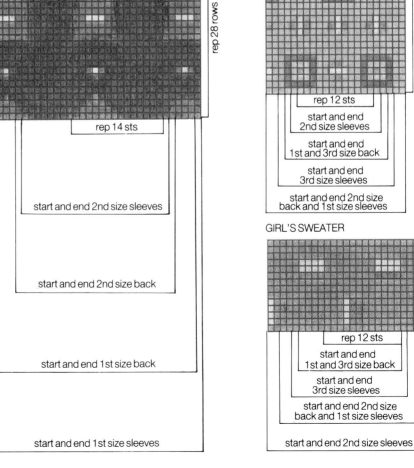

rep 14 rows

rep 12 sts

start and end
1st and 3rd size back

start and end
3rd size sleeves

start and end 2nd size
back and 1st size sleeves

start and end 2nd size sleeves

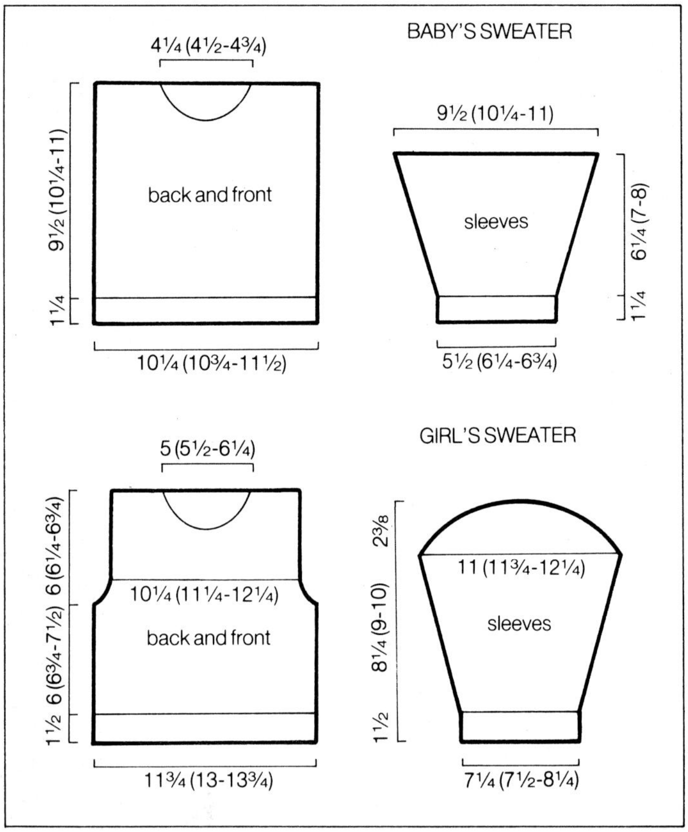
BABY'S SWEATER
4¼ (4½-4¾)
9½ (10¼-11)
1¼
back and front
10¼ (10¾-11½)
9½ (10¼-11)
sleeves
6¼ (7-8)
1¼
5½ (6¼-6¾)
GIRL'S SWEATER
5 (5½-6¼)
6 (6¼-6¾)
6 (6¾-7½)
1½
10¼ (11¼-12¼)
back and front
11¾ (13-13¾)
2⅜
8¼ (9-10)
1½
11 (11¾-12¼)
sleeves
7¼ (7½-8¼)

shaping until work measures 22½(23⅝)in/(57,60cm), ending with a k row.

▦ **Shoulder Shaping** Bind off 11 sts at beg of next and foll alt row, then 12 (15) sts at beg of foll alt row. Leave rem 23 (24) sts on a holder for neckband. Rejoin yarn to center back edge of right back sts and patt to end. Cont to match first side, reversing all shaping.

▦ **Front** Work as given for back to **. Inc 1 st at both ends of next and foll 4th row. Work 1 row straight.

▦ **Neck Shaping** *Next row* Patt 46 (49), turn and leave rem sts on a spare needle. Cont on these 46 (49) sts now rem on needle for left front; bind off at neck edge 3 sts at beg of next and 2 foll alt rows, 2 sts at beg of foll 3 alt rows, then 1 st at beg of foll alt row; *at the same time* inc 1 st at armhole edge on every 4th row as set to match back until 6 sts in all have been inc at this edge. 34 (37) sts. Cont without shaping until work measures the same as back to shoulders, ending with a p row.

▦ **Shoulder Shaping** Bind off 11 sts at beg of next and foll alt row. Work 1 row straight, then bind off rem 12 (15) sts. Return to sts on spare needle, slip first 15 (17) sts on to a holder for neckband, rejoin yarns to neck edge of right front sts, bind off 3 sts and patt to end. Cont to match first side, reversing all shaping.

▦ **Sleeves** With smaller needles and **A** cast on 53 (57) sts and work in rib as on back ribbing for 2in (5cm), ending with a 2nd rib row and inc 8 sts evenly across the last row. 61 (65) sts. Change to larger needles. Beg with a k row work in st st. Cont in patt from chart, inc 1 st at both ends of the 5th and every foll 6th row until there are 83 (93) sts, then every foll 4th row until there are 91 (95) sts. Cont without shaping until work measures 15⅜(16⅛)in/(39,41cm) from beg, ending with a p row.

▦ **Top Shaping** Keeping patt correct, bind off 4 sts at beg of next 2 rows, 3 sts at beg of next 4 rows, 2 sts at beg of next 12 rows, 1 st at beg of next 10 (12) rows, then 2 sts at beg of next 4 rows. Bind off rem 29 (31) sts.

▦ **Neckband** Join shoulder seams. With smaller needles, **A** and right side facing, pick up and k 92 (96) sts evenly round neck edge including sts on holders. Beg with a p row, work in st st. Work 2 rows, dec 6 sts evenly across the last row. 86 (90) sts. Work 7 more rows in **A**, 1 row in **B**, then 7 rows in **A**. Bind off *loosely*.

▦ **Finishing** At this stage darn in all loose ends. Sew in sleeves. Join side and sleeve seams. Fold neckband to inside on contrast line and sew in place.

▦ With crochet hook, **B** and right side facing, work 1 row in slip st along back neck opening, making 2 button loops. Fasten off. Sew on buttons.

BABY'S SWEATER

CHECKLIST

Materials

La Droguerie Tweed: 100(100-100)g of rose (**A**). *Surnaturelle: 20g each of rose* (**B**), *apricot and pale green. Pair each of needles size 2 and 7; small size crochet hook; 1 pink button.*

Sizes

Three sizes, to fit a baby aged 12 (18-24) months. Actual measurements shown on diagram.

Stitches used and gauge

As for Man's cardigan.

INSTRUCTIONS

▦ **Back** With smaller needles and **A**, cast on 65 (69-73) sts and work in rib as on back ribbing of Man's cardigan until work measures 1¼in (3cm) from beg, ending with a 2nd rib row. Change to larger needles and beg with a k row work in st st. Cont in patt from chart until work measures 10⅝(11⅜, 12¼)in/(27,29,31cm) from beg, ending with a p row. Bind off.

▦ **Front** Work as given for back unit front measures 9(9⅞,10⅝)in/(23,25,27cm) from beg, ending with a p row.

▦ **Neck Shaping** *Next row* Patt 27 (28-29) and leave these sts of left front on a spare needle, bind off next 11 (13-15) sts, patt to end. Cont on 27 (28-29) sts now rem on needle for right front; work 1 row straight. Bind off at neck edge 3 sts at beg of next row and foll alt row, then 2 sts at beg of foll alt row. 19 (20-21) sts.

▦ Cont without shaping until work measures the same as back to shoulders, ending with a p row. Bind off. Rejoin yarns to sts of left front, bind off 3 sts and patt to end. Cont to match first side, reversing shaping.

▦ **Sleeves** With smaller needles and **A** cast on 35 (39-43) sts and work in rib as on back ribbing for 1¼in (3cm), ending with a 2nd rib row. Change to larger needles and beg with a k row work in st st. Cont in patt from chart, inc 1 st at both ends of the 3rd and every other row until there are 61 (65-69) sts. Cont without shaping until work measures 7½(8¼,9)in/(19,21,23cm) from beg, ending with a p row. Bind off *loosely*.

▦ **Neckband** Join left shoulder seam. With smaller needles, **A** and right side facing, pick up and k 89 (95-101) sts evenly round neck edge. Beg with a 2nd row, work ¾in (2cm) in rib as on back. Bind off in rib.

▦ **Finishing** At this stage darn in all loose ends. Join right shoulder seam, leaving an opening at neck edge. On each side edge mark a

point 4¾(5⅛-5½)in/ (12,13,14cm) down from shoulder seams for armholes and sew bound-off edge of sleeves between marked points. Join side and sleeve seams.

▦ With crochet hook, **B** and right side facing, work 1 row in slip st along neck opening, making a button loop. Sew on button to match.

GIRL'S SWEATER

CHECKLIST

Materials
La Droguerie Tweed: *130(140-150)g of orange (**A**), and 20g of green. La Droggucric* Surnaturclle: *20g of palc ycllow. Pair each of needles size 2 and 7.*

Sizes
Three sizes, to fit ages 1/2 (2/3-4/5) years. Actual measurements shown on diagram.

Stitches used and gauge
As for Man's cardigan.

INSTRUCTIONS

▦ **Back** With smaller needles and **A** cast on 75 (81-87) sts and work in rib as on back ribbing of Man's cardigan for 1½in (4cm) ending with a 2nd rib row and inc 1 st in center of last row, 76 (82-88) sts. Change to larger needles and beg with a k row work in st st. Cont in patt from chart until work measures 7½(8¼,9)in/ (19,21,23cm) from beg, ending with a p row.

▦ **Armhole Shaping** Keeping patt correct, bind off 2 sts at beg of next 4 rows, then 1 st at beg of next 2 rows. 66 (72-78) sts. Cont without shaping until work measures 13⅜(14½,15¾)in/ (34,37,40cm) from beg, ending with a p row. Bind off.

▣ **Front** Work as given for back until front measures 11⅜(12⅝, 13¾)in/(29,32,35cm) from beg, ending with a p row.
▣ **Neck Shaping** *Next row* Patt 26 (27-28) and leave these sts of left front on a spare needle, bind off next 14 (18-22) sts, patt to end. Cont on 26 (27-28) sts now rem on needle for right front; work 1 row straight. Bind off at neck edge 3 sts at beg of next row, then every other row once, and then 2 sts every other row once, and 1 st once.
▣ Cont without shaping until work measures the same as back to shoulders, ending with a p row. Bind off. Rejoin yarns to neck edge of left front sts, bind off 3 sts and patt to end. Cont to match first side, reversing shaping.

▣ **Sleeves** With smaller needles and **A** cast on 45 (49-53) sts and work in rib as on back ribbing for 1½in (4cm) ending with a 2nd rib row and inc 1 st in center of last row. 46 (50-54) sts. Change to larger needles and beg with a k row work in st st. Cont in patt from chart, inc 1 st at both ends of the 3rd and every foll 4th row until there are 70 (74-78) sts. Cont without shaping until work measures 9⅞(10⅝,11⅜)in/ (25,27,29cm) from beg, ending with a p row.
▣ **Top Shaping** Keeping patt

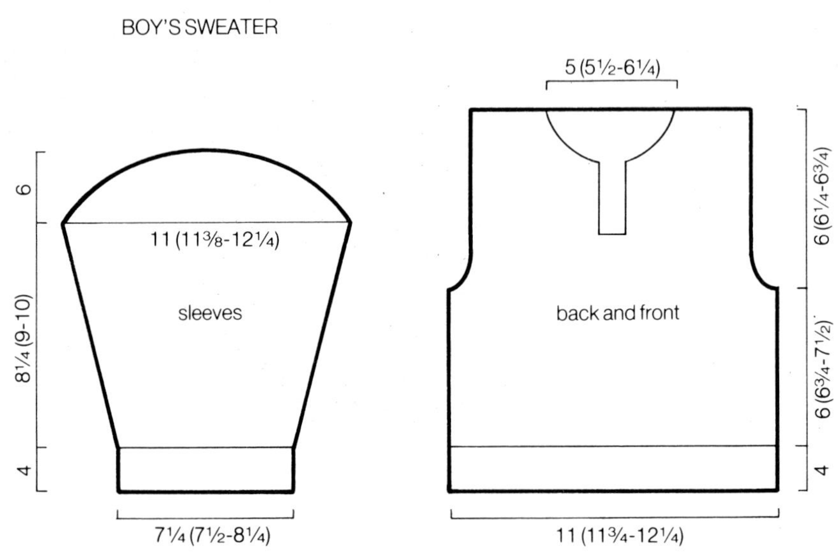

BOY'S SWEATER

CHECKLIST

Materials
La Droguerie Tweed: *170(190-200)g of blue* (**A**). Surnaturelle: *20g each of apricot, pale yellow* (**B**) *and pale green. Pair each of needles size 2 and 7; small crochet hook; 2 green buttons.*

Sizes
As for Girl's sweater.

Stitches used and gauge
As for Man's cardigan.

---

correct, bind off 4 sts at beg of next 4 rows, 2 sts at beg of next 6 rows, then 3 sts at beg of next 6 rows. Bind off rem 24 (28-32) sts.

▣ **Neckband** Join left shoulder seam. With smaller needles, **A** and right side facing, pick up and k 99 (107-115) sts evenly along neck edge. Beg with a 2nd row, work ¾in (2cm) in rib as on back ribbing. Bind off *loosely* in rib.

▣ **Finishing** At this stage darn in all loose ends. Join right shoulder and neckband seam. Sew in sleeves. Join side and sleeve seams.

BOY'S SWEATER

11 (11⅜-12¼)

sleeves

6

8¼ (9-10)

4

7¼ (7½-8¼)

5 (5½-6¼)

back and front

6 (6¼-6¾)

6 (6¾-7½)

4

11 (11¾-12¼)

INSTRUCTIONS

▣ **Back and Sleeves** Work as given for Girl's sweater.

▣ **Front** Work as given for back until front measures 9(9⅞,10⅝)in/ (23,25,27cm) from beg, ending with a p row.
▣ **Divide for Opening** *Next row* Patt 30 (33-36) and leave these sts of left front on a spare needle, bind off next 6 sts, patt to end. Cont on 30 (33-36) sts now rem on needle for right front; cont until work measures 11⅜(12⅝,13¾)in/ (29,32,35cm) from beg, ending with a p row.
▣ **Neck Shaping** Keeping patt correct, bind off at neck edge 4 (6-8) sts at beg of next row, 4 sts at every other row once, 3 sts every other row once, then 2 sts once, 17 (18-19) sts. Cont without shaping until work measures the same as back to shoulders, ending with a p row. Bind off. Rejoin yarns to left front sts and patt to end. Cont to match first side, reversing shaping.
▣ **Collar** With smaller needles and **A** cast on 99 (107-115) sts and work in rib as on back ribbing

until work measures 2⅜in (6cm) from beg. Bind off *loosely* in rib.

▣ **Button Band** With smaller needles and **A** cast on 11 sts and work in rib as on back ribbing until band, when slightly stretched, reaches up front opening. Bind off in rib. Tack band in place, with pins mark position of buttons, first to come ¾in (2cm) from cast on edge and 2nd to come ⅜in (1cm) from bound off edge.
▣ **Buttonhole Band** Work as given for button band, making buttonholes to correspond with positions of pins as foll: (right side) rib 4, bind off next 3 sts, rib 4.
▣ *Next row* Rib to end, casting on 3 sts over the 3 bind off.

▣ **Finishing** At this stage darn in all loose ends. Join shoulder seams. Sew in sleeves. Join side and sleeve seams. Sew on front bands, sewing cast on edges to cast off sts at center front. Sew cast on edge of collar to neck edge, beginning and ending in center of front bands. With crochet hook, **B** and right side facing, work 1 row in slip st along edges of front bands and collar. Fasten off. Sew on buttons.

YARN OPTIONS

Heads in the Clouds

Young Shrimpers

Some of the speciality yarns used in this book are not readily available outside France, but this should not deter you from knitting any of the patterns. In all cases, we suggest either acceptable substitutes which will knit to the same tension as the original or, if there is one, list the main stockist for that type of yarn (see overleaf). In some cases, the stockist may not always be able to supply the particular yarn used, in which case we give the address of the stockist and at the same time suggest a substitute yarn.

Heads in the Clouds *Substitute Georges Picaud* Feu Vert *for* Shetland, *and Georges Picaud* Zig *for* Orient Express.

Young Shrimpers Coton *Sophie Desroches – see overleaf for stockist.*

Snow Set *Jacket with Roll Collar in Anny Blatt* Soft'Anny Kid Mohair, *see overleaf for stockist.*
Jacket with Revers in Bouton d'Or Mohair Gratté, *substitute Bouton d'Or* Pur Mohair 100, *see overleaf for stockist.*
Parka in Laine Plassard Florès, *substitute Anny Blatt* Soft'Anny Kid Mohair, *see overleaf for stockist.*
Child's Jacket in Berger du Nord Kid Mohair, *see overleaf for stockist.*
Scarf and other accessories in Laine Plassard Florès, *substitute Anny Blatt* Soft'Anny Kid Mohair.

Negative/Positive *If you are unable to obtain the yarn stated, we suggest that you substitute a fine baby yarn such as 3 Suisses* Lucky Baby *or 3 Suisses* Sweet Baby. *If you would like to keep to the original color scheme, use 3 Suisses* Suizanyl, *which is*

Animal Magic

Comforting Mohair

Snow Set

obtainable in black as well as white.

Animal Magic *Fox* and *Cat in Laine de la Droguerie* Mohair, *substitute 3 Suisses* New Mohair 3S. *Lamb in Laine de la Droguerie* Igloo, *substitute 3 Suisses* Kalinka, *used* double.

Mouse in Laine de la Droguerie Mohair *and* Angora, *substitute 3 Suisses* New Mohair 3S *for both yarns.*

Gym Tonic *Substitute Pingouin* Sorbet *for Laine de la Droguerie* Fluo.

Lightning Flash *For Laine Marigold* 4 fils, *substitute either Pingouin* Pingofine *or Pingouin* Pingolaine.

Comforting Mohair *See overleaf for stockist.*

Scandinavian Snowflakes *Sleeping Bag, Man's Sweater and Girl's Sweater in Laine Marigold* 4 fils, *substitute 3 Suisses* Lanasport Nina Ricci.

Girl's Scarf in Laine Marigold 3 fils, *substitute 3 Suisses* Sweet Lady *and size 3 needles.*

Woman and Child's Scarf and Woman and Child's Sweater in Malourène Elk, *substitute 3 Suisses* Super Lana Yves St Laurent.

Country Kids *Style 1 in Novita* Florica, *substitute Pingouin* Pingofine *as follows:*
*No 330, Giroselle (**A**); No 416, Flamme (**B**); No 331, Feu (**C**); No 392, Aube (**D**); No 335, Pouissin (**E**), and No 313, Nuage (**F**).*
Style 2 in Novita Florica, *substitute Pingouin* Pingofine *as follows:*
*No 352, Dune (**A**); No 424, Cuivre (**B**); No 416, Flamme (**C**); No 331, Feu (**D**); No 422, Coralline (**E**); No 406, Eucalyptus (**F**), and No 381, Griotte (**G**).*
Style 3 in Novita Fauna, *substitute Pingouin* Pingostar *as follows:*
*No 602, Saigon (**A**); No 511, Hawai (**B**); No 513, Nuage (**C**); No 528, Bleu Franc (**D**) and No 529, Amiral (**E**).*
In the original instructions **E** *is used double as it is a thinner yarn, but there is no need to do this if you are substituting Pingouin* Pingostar *for all the colors.*

Tweedy Family *Substitute 3 Suisses* Morocco *and size 5 needles.*

Tweedy Family

Scandinavian Snowflakes

Country Kids

Animal Magic

Gym Tonic

STOCKISTS

If you have difficulty obtaining the specified yarns in your area, the stockists listed below may be able to help you, either by supplying the yarn directly to you or by giving you the name of your local supplier.

BERGER DU NORD
Brookman & Sons Inc., 4416 North East 11th Avenue, Fort Lauderdale, Florida 33334

GEORGES PICAUD YARNS USA
Merino Wool Co. Inc., 230 Fifth Avenue, Suite 2000, New York, NY 10001 Tel. 212-686-0050

LAINES ANNY BLATT INC
24770 Crestview Court, Farmington Hills, Michigan 48018 Tel. 313-474-2942

PINGOUIN
Promofil Corp (USA), 9179 Red Branch Road, Columbia, Maryland 21045 Tel. 301-730-0101

3 SUISSES
Dominique Corp., Empire State Building, Suite 2709, 350 Fifth Avenue, New York, NY 10018